Young People, Social Capital and Ethnic Identity

Social capital and ethnicity are crucial to young people's understandings of their social world. The strong bonding networks often assumed in ethnic groups suggest that individuals may prefer to be bonded to each other according to shared socio-cultural factors such as shared histories, memories, language, customs, traditions and values. However, bridging forms of social capital allow new understandings of ethnic identities to emerge, and which involve dynamic and complex social processes that are continually changing and evolving according to time, location and context.

This book explores the ways in which the concepts of social capital and ethnicity play a central role in young people's relationships, participation in wider social networks and the construction of identities. Researchers and scholars working in the fields of children and youth studies, education, families, social and racial and ethnic studies, offer differing accounts of the ways in which social capital operates in young people's lives across diverse social settings and ethnic groups. This edited book is timely and significant given the public interest of researchers, academics, politicians and policy-makers working in areas of youth and community work, race relations and cultural diversity.

This book was published as a special issue of *Ethnic and Racial Studies*.

Tracey Reynolds is a Senior Research Fellow at the Families and Social Capital Research Group, London South Bank University.

Contents

Notes on Contributors

Ravinder Barn is Professor in the Department of Health and Social Care at Royal Holloway, University of London.

Daniel Briggs is a Senior Lecturer in Criminology and Criminal Justice at the University of East London.

Arniika Kuusisto is Researcher in the Department of Applied Sciences of Education at the University of Helsinki.

Sheena Mcgrellis is a Senior Research Fellow in the Families and Social Capital Research Group, London South Bank University, but based at University of Ulster, Magee.

Tracey Reynolds is Senior Research Fellow in the Families and Social Capital Research Group, at London South Bank University.

Susie Weller is a Senior Research Fellow in the Families & Social Capital Research Group at London South Bank University.

Elisabetta Zontini is Lecturer in the School of Sociology and Social Policy at Nottingham University.

Editorial introduction: young people, social capital and ethnic identity

Tracey Reynolds

Abstract

British empirical analyses investigating the relationship between ethnicity and social capital tend to highlight the views and experiences of adult minority ethnic individuals. In contrast the experiences of young people remain an under developed, but growing, research area. Our interest in this special issue stems from the desire to promote young people's voices in public and policy debates, particularly those from minority ethnic groups and communities, and to bring to the fore their experiences. Drawing on empirical research conducted in the Caribbean, England, Finland, Italy and Northern Ireland, the collection of articles explores the social capital of young people across diverse ethnic and cultural settings. We draw on theories of ethnicity and social capital to explore the ways in which they might be utilised as social resources by young people. We consider how ethnicity and cultural belonging might be regarded as both positive and negative forms of social capital among young people. We also critically reflect on ideas about social capital and ethnicity to assess the extend to which new forms of identities, networks and participation are emerging in the real life contexts of young people belonging to cultural and ethnic minority communities.

In recent times the concepts of ethnicity and social capital have attracted much policy attention both nationally and internationally. Researchers and policy-makers in a variety of different fields have focused on the relationship between ethnicity and social capital to provide generalized explanations of rapid social changes occurring in contemporary western societies, and also to reflect on whether these changes have been for the good or ill (Goulbourne and Solomos 2003).

Ethnicity and social capital analyses also address the collective networks that emerge from individuals and groups sharing a common set of values (Cheong *et al.* 2005). British empirical analyses investigating the relationship between ethnicity and social capital tend to highlight the views and experiences of adult minority ethnic individuals. In contrast, the experiences of young people remain an under-developed research area. Although there have been growing number of studies that examine social capital and ethnicity in relation to young people (see, for example, Dwyer *et al.* 2006; Parker and Song 2006; Reynolds 2006a, 2000b), this is countered by studies that either marginalize the experiences of young people or contextualize them as objects of study. Indeed, young people across ethnically and culturally diverse groups are typically recognized as passive beneficiaries or recipients of social capital (Morrow 2001; Weller 2006; Holland, Reynolds and Weller 2007). A number of writers focusing on children and young people are also critical of the way in which the literature constructs them as competitors for resources rather than individuals generating social capital in their own right (Holloway and Valentine 2000; Gillies and Lucey 2006).

Our interest in this special issue stems from the desire to promote young people's voices in public and policy debates, particularly those from minority ethnic groups and communities, and to bring to the fore their experiences. The collection of articles in this social issue volume emerged out of a one-day conference entitled 'Young People, Ethnicity and Social Capital', organized as part of the Families and Social Capital Research Group seminar series, and held at London South Bank University in March 2008. Drawing on empirical research conducted in the Caribbean, England, Finland, Italy and Northern Ireland, the collection of articles explores the social capital of young people across diverse ethnic and cultural settings. Crucially, we draw on theories of ethnicity and social capital to explore the ways in which they might be utilized as social resources by young people. Our discussion also considers how ethnicity and cultural belonging might be regarded as both positive and negative forms of social capital among young people. We similarly reflect critically on ideas about social capital and ethnicity to assess the extent to which new forms of identities, networks and participation are emerging in the real-life contexts of young people belonging to cultural and ethnic minority communities. This editorial introduction begins with a brief overview of the main theories of social capital and ethnicity. While the aim of this discussion is not to analyse the extensive literature and debates on these theories, it is important to highlight how they have conceptually guided our analyses.

Contextualizing social capital and ethnicity

Social capital has become an increasingly popular and influential concept in policy debates and social theory, both nationally and internationally. Various writers have constructed and applied the idea of social capital in different ways, but it is broadly understood as 'the values that people hold and the resources that they can access, which both result in and are the result of collective and socially negotiated ties and relationships' (Edwards, Franklin and Holland 2003, p. 2). Uniting the differentiated accounts of social capital is the assumption that people often develop networks and group membership with others who have a shared set of norms and values. Theories of social capital are primarily concerned with understanding the processes, relationships and resources which emerge from, and result in, social networks or group membership. The qualities of individuals' social relationships and the conditions that create individuals' social networks have long been a concern of James Coleman (1990) and Robert Putnam (2000), two eminent social capital theorists. Both writers highlight the importance of resources, which are reproduced and made available to individuals in social networks. Putnam's work, however, emphasizes notions of trust, reciprocity and civic engagement as particular forms of social capital generated in social networks. The significance of strong civic association and participation lies in its potential for developing social integration and social cohesion. In particular, Putnam's (1994) theoretical framework highlights that social capital is differentiated according to its capacity to produce 'bonding' and 'bridging' networks. 'Bonding' social capital is characterized by its inward-looking and clannish nature. It promotes relationships and networks of trust and reciprocity that reinforce bonds and connections within homogenous groups. 'Bridging' social capital, in contrast, is outward looking and involves building connections, relationships and networks of trust and reciprocity between heterogeneous groups and communities.[1] Coleman (1990) adopts a functionalist approach to understanding social capital. He contends that families and communities are used as a social resource by individuals to best represent their interests and achieve social mobility. In essence, social capital is a desired resource that mutually benefits both individuals and their family and community members. Strong social capital is a result of strong family and community relations, a shared set of norms and values and the normative expectation of obligation and reciprocity.

Both Putnam's and Coleman's approaches to social capital have been criticized on a number of issues. For example, Coleman's work has been criticized for his failure to theorize between 'strong' and 'weak' ties and his essentialist constructions of family and community (Portes 1998). Similarly, both writers have been criticized for their failure to acknowledge the ways in which power and structural inequalities are reproduced in social networks, including ethnic, gender and social-class inequalities (Morrow 2001; Edwards and Gillies 2005; Goulbourne 2006).

Pierre Bourdieu (1997), a third main contributor to the development of social capital theory, is often discussed as a 'corrective' in discourses of social capital (Holland, Reynolds and Weller 2007). His work establishes the connections between power, ideology and structural inequality in wider society. With his integrative typology of capitals (economic, social, cultural and symbolic), Bourdieu (1986) argues that social capital is deployed in the reproduction of social-class privilege and inequality. His critical analysis details the connections and intertwined relationships emerging from different forms of capital that constitute people's position in the social order. Social capital serves to reproduce inequalities, but cultural and economic capitals are also integral to this process. Bourdieu's work is particularly instrumental in understanding how individuals belonging to subordinate groups might improve their socio-economic status by deploying and investing in a range of different capitals.

Although ethnicity (alongside gender) is rarely, if ever, explicitly referred to by Putnam, Coleman and Bourdieu, it could be argued that many of their key ideas provide a theoretical basis for thinking about the relationship between ethnicity and social capital, particularly in relation to culturally and ethnically diverse young people. In Britain, for example, the changing patterns of immigration, specific instances of ethnic tensions and social unrest in Northern Ireland and other English towns and cities (e.g. the Brixton riots in the 1980s) and widespread concerns about the increased numbers of asylum seekers and refugees entering Britain have brought issues of ethnic diversity and social cohesion to the forefront of public and media debates. Much of the interest has centred on the negative impact of ethnic diversity on social cohesion and civic participation, and the need to instil a core set of values among diverse ethnic and racial groups to foster solidarity (McGhee 2003; Goodhart 2004).

The highly politicized and emotive rhetoric framing media and policy debates of ethnicity and social capital has resulted in limited interest in understanding how ethnicity and ethnic identification influence social capital processes, and also the various ways in which ethnically and culturally diverse individuals, families and communities negotiate understandings of social capital in their everyday lives. Ethnicity as a theoretical concept is commonly explained in relation to race, class, age, gender, religion, culture and nationhood (Evergeti and Zontini 2006). Theories of ethnicity explore the dynamics of social change and the maintenance of social boundaries (Barth 1969). In seeking to theorize ethnicity in relation to social capital the social boundaries between indigenous and ethnic 'other' communities are sometimes constructed as impenetrable and enduring in multi-ethnic societies (Goulbourne 2002). Moreover, the strong bonding networks that characterize ethnic groupings suggests that individuals usually prefer to remain within groups with shared socio-cultural factors such as common histories, memories, language, customs, traditions and values (Zhou 2005). Government policy in the UK is particularly interested in the changing nature of black and minority ethnic communities originating from other European states, the Caribbean, Africa and South Asian communities, and more recently refugees and asylum seekers from Eastern Europe and Middle Eastern territories, in terms of the impact of these ethnic groups on the core values of British national identity (Home Office 2001). The concerns have centred on the crisis of social cohesion in Britain and the perception that particular ethnic groups and communities demonstrate a lack of willingness to participate in civic and associational life (Faulkner 2004; Fevre 2004; Runnymede Trust 2004). Studies conducted by Parekh (2000) and Ousley (2001) concerning this relationship between ethnic diversity and community cohesion suggest that the comparative failure of different racial-ethnic groups to integrate and work together to resolve common concerns contributed to social unrest in the northern English towns of Burnley and Oldham and the city of Bradford in 2001. Although the desire for social integration has prompted policy-makers to focus on improving the involvement of minority ethnic communities in civic participation and the democratic decision-making process, there still exists concern that increased ethnic diversity will erode existing social capital resources and ties of trust and reciprocal obligation within local communities and wider society (Cheong *et al.* 2005).

Concerns about the loss and erosion of social capital with ethnic diversity suggest that social capital is typically understood to be a positive resource that individuals, families and communities can employ to best serve their own interests. Within debates there is a tendency to idealize the positive aspects of social capital in terms of the production of strong group networks and also to emphasize its protective factors for ethnic identity development. The negative side of social capital for individuals and community remains largely unexplored territory. However, the possibility that young people may encounter negative social capital is examined in this special issue. Elisabetta Zontini's article, for example, considers the extent to which social capital resources generated in Italian family and community networks restrict young people's freedom to choose their own lifestyles. Similarly, Daniel Briggs' discussion examines how negative social capital might encourage minority ethnic youths, living in disadvantaged communities, to identify strongly with criminal gangs and in turn lead to increased incidences of crime and mistrust within the local communities. Finally, Ravinder Barn's article contends that a further potential risk factor of bonding social capital is that minority ethnic young people who are already vulnerable in the care system when leaving care may internalize racism and feel ill-equipped to develop a positive sense of self and racial-ethnic identity.

In a more general sense, social capital helps to reinforce the unequal power relations that exist within ethnic groups. Feminist scholars have highlighted gendered, and generational, power relations that exist within ethnically diverse families and communities (Molyneaux 2001; Zontini 2007). Social class continues to determine inequality in accessing resources and capitals between middle- and working-class individuals (Skeggs 2003; Gillies 2007), and interrelated issues of race and racism also produce structural inequalities for minority ethnic groups. This issue of unequal power relations is clearly obvious between children/young people and adults, especially within the context of families and education services (Schaefer-McDaniel 2004). What is less clear, however, is the way in which intersections of race, class, gender and age create unequal power differentials among young people themselves.

Young people, ethnicity and social capital

It has been argued that the work of influential social capital theorists, such as Coleman, Putnam and Bourdieu fails to account for the active role of children and young people in the creation and maintenance of social capital within families and communities (Schaefer-McDaniel 2004; Weller forthcoming). A number of studies concerned with young people highlight their ability to influence social networks and to deploy social capital resources to suit their own ends (Morrow 2001; Leonard 2005; Helve and Bynner 2007; Holland 2008).

'Youth-oriented' accounts are particularly relevant to debates on social capital and ethnicity because adolescence and young adulthood are crucial phases in the life-course where individuals begin to explore issues of identity formation, separate from their family and parents (Morrow 1999; Lucey and Reay 2000; Helve 2007). With regard to minority ethnic young people, part of this identity-making is articulated in ethnic-racial terms, and involves them developing an 'ethnic self' within the context of ethnic and cultural diversity (Reynolds 2007). The shifting circumstances of late modernity, including, for example, the rise in immigration, social and geographical mobility, single-parent households and single-dwelling households, has also fostered concerns about self-identity and individuals' right to choose their own lifestyles (Weeks, Donovan and Heaphy 2001). With the emphasis on individuals' needs and personal freedom, it has been argued that non-kinship networks are becoming more salient than blood relatives in defining who we are as individuals (Pahl and Pevalin

2005). Yet, the various contributions to this special issue recognize that young people's non-kinship networks are shaped by a number of intersecting factors, including membership of family ties, neighbourhood and community, shared sets of norms and values, and also schooling and migration (Goulbourne *et al.* 2010).

Several discussions in this volume, particularly those by Sheena McGrellis, Arniika Kuusisto and Tracey Reynolds, are interested in understanding how young people's identities are influenced by their real or symbolic attachment to geographical communities (e.g. local neighbourhood, region and familial country of origin), social communities (e.g. schools, religious groups and gangs) and the cultural norms and values of these communities.

The discussion by Susie Weller identifies that young people with a strong attachment to their local schools and neighbourhoods are more likely to interact with peers, make friends and build social networks from across racial and ethnic diverse groups. Our exploration of bridging forms of social capital in young people's lives allows new understandings of ethnic identities to emerge. For example, Sheena McGrellis's article highlights that young people growing in Northern Ireland during the era of sectarian violence, and then the 'peace process', responded to these political and social changes by crossing boundaries and generating inter-community contact. We also demonstrate the particular ways that transnational communities create similar networks of trust and reciprocity for young people across nation-states (see Reynolds and Zontini in this volume).

Themes of this issue

In this special issue the dominant paradigms about social capital among culturally and ethnically diverse young people are questioned through the interrelated themes of divided and diverse communities, migration and transnational family networks, social care and well-being, and the complexity of young people's identities and networks. The articles also explore the cultural and social contexts in which young people operate and the use of social capital in developing identity.

The first two papers focus on divided and diverse communities. Sheena McGrellis considers the turbulent history of Northern Ireland, which has created communities that display high levels of intra-community trust and localized networking associated with bonding social capital. The political and social changes brought about by the 'peace process' have created possibilities for greater inter-community contact and potential for the generation of bridging social capital. Growing up in this period of transition young people in the 'Inventing Adulthoods' study have been affected by and responded to these changes, and to the experience of sectarianism and violence, in different ways. This paper explores the biographical journeys of a small number of these young people from 1996 to 2006, and considers how ethnic and territorial boundaries have shaped the social and spatial fabric of their lives. It asks to what extent and how young people growing up in spaces characterized by networks, values and social relationships that are indicative of bonding social capital, can straddle boundaries and challenge the processes of social and class reproduction.

Arniika Kuusisto explores how young people growing up in families affiliated with a religious minority negotiate their religious values and social identity in the social contexts of minority and majority. Although these young people belong to the ethnic majority in Finland, the religious and lifestyle values of their home and religious community differ from the Lutheran mainstream, which causes discrepancies between the values of their socialization background and those of their peer group. The negotiations of values and identities are here examined through examples of the teenagers' interview data. These examples illustrate the varied strategies for negotiation, positive versus negative experiences on the acquired negotiation outcomes, as well as the diversity within a minority community and the different ways of being a member of a religious minority.

In the subsequent two papers on migration and transnational family networks, the article by Tracey Reynolds explores the issue of transnational family relationships and return migration among British-Caribbean second-generation young people. She describes how transnational family ties and social networks are utilized as social capital resources to facilitate these young people's migration from Britain to the Caribbean, their parents' country of origin. A combination of internally formed and externally imposed understandings of ethnic identity, home and belonging are also important factors influencing these young people's decision to migrate to the Caribbean. Drawing on in-depth interviews with a qualitative sample of second-generation return migrants residing in Jamaica, the discussion reflects on how these young people manage their adjustment and settlement. It also explores the gendered nature of their experiences of return migration.

Elisabetta Zontini's article sets out to examine the use, production and maintenance of social capital in the context of migration through an in-depth analysis of the everyday experiences of young people in Italian families in the UK and Italy. Social capital is usually described in the literature as membership in networks that either helps individuals to get ahead or to preserve positions of power. In this article, Elisabetta moves beyond these one-sided understandings of social capital by exploring both the positive and negative traits of family and ethnic solidarity as specific forms of social capital for Italian young people. By focusing on the experiences of Italian young people the analysis also demonstrates that gender and generation are crucial axes for interpreting different experiences in participating in strong family and ethnic networks.

Social care and well-being is the focus of the next two papers. Ravinder Barn examines the issue of racial identity and social capital among care leavers. She highlights that young people leaving state care are recognized to be one of the most marginalized groups in society. In comparison to their counterparts living with their own family and community context, care leavers experience enormous adversity and upheaval. A combination of poor pre-care, in-care and post-care experiences serves to disadvantage this group of young people in many important ways. Moreover, research evidence documents the complexity of identity issues and concerns for minority ethnic children and young people who are separated from their birth families and are being brought up in public care. By drawing upon a recent and wider empirical study into care leavers in England, this paper explores the sociological concept of social capital and the ways in which this may contribute to young people's understanding and negotiation of their own racial and ethnic identity.

In his study of minority ethnic youths living in economically deprived areas of inner-London, Daniel Briggs explores the way in which minority ethnic young people can be equipped to develop social capital resources to counter the powerful social and structural forces which expose them to 'street life' and involvement in crime and gangs. Daniel's discussion is based on his evaluation of a mentoring programme designed to raise the self-esteem of 'at risk' youths and deter their participation in gangs and violent crime. The paper, first, applies a brief contextual understanding of urban minority ethnic young people's experiences of school and 'street life'. It then describes the background and aims of the mentoring programme in order to discuss how this has contributed to notions of trust, self-esteem, self-empowerment and identity among 'at risk' minority ethnic youths, and its impact on their social and family relationships.

Finally, Susie Weller focuses on the complexity of young people's identities and networks. Drawing on material from an ongoing longitudinal study, she addresses the relative neglect afforded to young people in dominant social capital debates. She argues that a nuanced and context-sensitive approach to the analysis of social capital is necessary in order to explore young people's complex identities and networks. While numerous policy-makers have drawn heavily on the work of influential theorist Robert Putnam, whose recent thinking has been implicated in debates concerning identity and diversity, what is meant by 'diversity' is subject to conjecture. Identities and affiliations are more complex than often presented in social capital debates. Acknowledging the significance of time and space, the paper explores the interface between different aspects of identity, 'community' affiliations and the dynamic nature of young people's social networks.

Acknowledgements

I would like to thank members of the Families and Social Capital Collective for their assistance with the special issue, particularly Susie Weller for her detailed revisions to earlier drafts and Janet Holland and Val Gillies for their feedback and comments. I would also like to thank the speakers and participants who attended the one-day conference on 'Young People, Ethnicity and Social Capital', held at London South Bank University in March 2008.

Note

1.   Michael Woolcock (1998) also describes 'linking' social capital as a third dimension. This involves the capacity of social capital to develop relationships and networks of trust and reciprocity that allow individuals to access and link across different formal and informal resources.

References

BARTH, FREDRIK 1969 *Ethnic Groups and Boundaries: The Social Organisation of Culture and Difference*, Boston, MA: Little Brown
BOURDIEU, PIERRE 1986 'The forms of capital', in J. G. Richardson (ed.), *Handbook of Theory and Research for Sociology of Education*, New York: Greenwood Press, pp. 214–258
――――― 1997 'The forms of capital', in A. H. Halsey, H. Lauder, P. Brown and A. S. Wells (eds), *Education: Culture, Economy, Society*, Oxford: Oxford University Press
CHEONG, PAULINE *et al.* 2005 'Immigration, social capital and social cohesion: a critical review', paper presented at the conference 'Whither Social Capital? Past, Present and Future', London South Bank University, 6–7 April
COLEMAN, JAMES 1990 *Foundations of Social Theory*, Cambridge, MA: Harvard University Press
DWYER, CLAIRE *et al.* 2006 'Ethnicity as social capital? Explaining the differential educational achievements of young British Pakistani men and women', paper presented at the 'Ethnicity, Mobility and Society' Leverhulme Programme Conference at University of Bristol, 16–17 March
EDWARDS, ROSALIND and GILLIES, VAL 2005 *Resources in Parenting: Access to Social Capital Project*, Families and Social Capital ESRC Research Group Working Paper Series, no. 14, London South Bank University
EDWARDS, ROSALIND, FRANKLIN, JANE and HOLLAND, JANET 2003 *Families and Social Capital: Exploring the Issues*, Families & Social Capital ESRC Research Group Working Paper Series, No. 1, London South Bank University
EVERGETI, VENETIA and ZONTINI, ELISABETTA 2006 'Introduction: some critical reflections on social capital, migration and transnational families', *Ethnic and Racial Studies*, vol. 29, no. 6, pp. 1025–39

FAULKNER, DAVID 2004 *Civil Renewal, Diversity and Social Capital in Multi-Ethnic Britain*, London: Runnymede Trust

FEVRE, RALPH 2004 'Social capital and the participation of marginalised groups in government', ESRC funded project R000249410

GILLIES, VAL 2007 *Marginalized Mothers: Exploring Working-Class Experiences of Parenting*, London: Routledge

GILLIES, VAL and LUCEY, HELEN 2006 '"It's a connection you can't get away from": brothers, sisters and social capital', *Journal of Youth Studies*, vol. 9, no. 4, pp. 479–93

GOODHART, DAVID 2004 'Too diverse?', *Prospect*, February

GOULBOURNE, HARRY 2002 *Caribbean Transnational Experience*, London: Pluto Press

—— 2006 'Editorial: families, minority ethnic communities and social capital in Britain', *Journal of Community, Work and Family*, vol. 9, no. 3, pp. 227–33

GOULBOURNE, HARRY and SOLOMOS, JOHN 2003 'Families, ethnicities and social capital', *Social Policy and Society*, vol. 2, no. 4, pp. 329–38

GOULBOURNE, HARRY, SOLOMOS, JOHN, REYNOLDS, TRACEY and ZONTINI, ELIZABETTA 2010 *Transnational Families*, London: Routledge

HELVE, HELENA 2007 'Social capital and minority identity', in H. Helve and J. Bynner (eds), *Youth and Social Capital*, London: Tufnell Press

HELVE, HELENA and BYNNER, JOHN (eds) 2007 *Youth and Social Capital*, London: Tufnell Press

HOLLAND, JANET 2008 *Young People and Social Capital: What Can It Do for Us?* Families & Social Capital ESRC Research Group Working Paper, No. 24, London: London South Bank University

HOLLAND, JANET, REYNOLDS, TRACEY and WELLER, SUSIE 2007 'Transitions, networks and communities: the significance of social capital in the lives of children and young people', *Journal of Youth Studies*, vol. 10, no. 1, pp. 97–116

HOLLOWAY, SUE and VALENTINE, GILL 2000 'Spatiality and the new social studies of childhood', *Sociology*, vol. 34, no. 4, pp. 763–83

HOME OFFICE 2001 *Community Cohesion: The Cantle Report*, London: HMSO

LEONARD, M. 2005 'Children, childhood and social capital: exploring the links', *Sociology*, vol. 39, no. 4, pp. 605–22

LUCEY, HELEN and REAY, DIANE 2000 'Identities in transition: anxiety and excitement in the move to secondary school', *Oxford Review of Education*, vol. 26, no. 2, pp. 191–205

MCGHEE, DEREK 2003 'Moving to a common ground: a critical examination of community cohesion discourse in the twenty-first century Britain', *The Sociological Review*, vol. 51, pp. 376–404

MOLYNEUX, MAXINE 2001 'Social capital: a post transition concept? Questions of context and gender from a Latin American perspective', in V. Morrow (ed.), *An Appropriate Capital-isation? Questioning Social Capital*, Research in Progress Series, Issue 1, London: Gender Institute, London School of Economics

MORROW, VIRGINIA (ed.) 1999 *An Appropriate Capital-isation? Questioning Social Capital*, Research in Progress Series, Issue 1, London: Gender Institute, London School of Economics

—— (ed.) 2001 'Conceptualising social capital in relation to the well-being of children and young people: a critical review', *Sociological Review*, vol. 47, no. 4, pp. 744–65

OUSLEY, HERMAN 2001 *Community Pride, Not Prejudice: Making Diversity Work in Bradford*, Bradford: Bradford Vision

PAHL, RAY and PEVALIN, DAVID 2004 'Between family and friends: a longitudinal study of friendship choice', *The British Journal of Sociology*, vol. 56, no. 3, pp. 433–50

PAREKH, BHIKHU 2000 *The Future of Multi-Cultural Britain*, London: Runnymede Trust

PARKER, DAVID and SONG, MIRI 2006 'Ethnicity, social capital and the internet: British Chinese websites', *Ethnicities*, vol. 6, no. 2, pp. 178–202

PORTES, ALEJANDRO 1998 'Social capital: its origin and applications in modern sociology', *Annual Review of Sociology*, vol. 24, no. 1, pp. 1–24

PUTNAM, ROBERT 1994 'Tuning in, turning out: the strange disappearance of social capital in America', *American Political Science Association Online*, http://www.apsanet.org/ps/dec95/putfig2.cfm
―――― 2000 *Bowling Alone: The Collapse and Revival of American Community*, New York: Simon & Schuster
REYNOLDS, TRACEY 2006a 'Caribbean young people, family relationships and social capital', *Journal of Ethnic and Racial Studies*, vol. 29, no. 6, pp. 1087–103
―――― 2006b 'Bonding social capital within the Caribbean family and community', *Journal of Community, Work and Family*, vol. 9, no. 3, pp. 273–90
―――― 2007 'Judged by the company we keep: friendships networks, social capital and ethnic identity of Caribbean young people in Britain', in H. Helve and J. Bynner (eds), *Youth and Social Capital*, London: Tufnell Press, pp. 71–86
RUNNYMEDE TRUST 2004 *Civic Renewal and Social Capital*, Runnymede Quarterly Bulletin, September
SCHAEFER-MCDANIEL, NINA J. 2004 'Conceptualizing social capital among young people: toward a new theory', *Children, Youth and Environments*, vol. 14, no. 1, pp. 140–50
SKEGGS, BEVERLEY 2003 *Class, Self and Culture*, London: Routledge
WEEKS, JEFFREY, DONOVAN, CATHERINE and HEAPHY, BRIAN 2001 'Everyday experiments: narratives of non-heterosexual relationships', in E. Silva and C. Smart (eds), *The New Family?*, London: Sage
WELLER, SUSIE 2007 'Managing the move to secondary school: the significance of children's social capital', in H. Helve and J. Bynner (eds), *Youth and Social Capital*, London: Tufnell Press, pp. 107–25
―――― forthcoming '"You need to have a mixed school ...": exploring the complexity of diversity in young people's social networks', in J. Allan, J. Ozga and G. Smyth (eds), *Social Capital, Professionalism and Diversity: New Relations in Urban Schools*, Rotterdam: Sense
WOOLCOCK, MICHAEL 1998 'Social capital and economic development: towards a theoretical synthesis and policy framework', *Theory and Society*, vol. 27, pp. 151–208
ZHOU, MIN 2005 'Ethnicity as social capital: community-based institutions and embedded networks of social relations', in G. Loury, T. Madood and S. Teles (eds), *Ethnicity, Social Mobility and Public Policy in the US and UK*, Cambridge: Cambridge University Press
ZONTINI, ELISABETTA 2007 'Continuities and change in transnational Italian families: the caring practices of second generation women', *Journal of Ethnic and Migration Studies*, vol. 33, no. 7, pp. 1103–19

In transition: young people in Northern Ireland growing up in, and out of, divided communities

Sheena McGrellis

Abstract

The history of Northern Ireland has created communities that display high levels of intra-community trust and localized networking associated with 'bonding' social capital. Political and social changes brought about by the 'peace process' have created possibilities for greater inter-community contact and potential for the generation of 'bridging' social capital. Growing up in this period of transition, young people in the *Inventing Adulthoods* study have been affected by and have responded to these changes, and to the experience of sectarianism and violence, in different ways. This paper explores the biographical journeys of a small number of young people from 1996 to 2006, and considers how ethnic and territorial boundaries have shaped the social and spatial fabric of their lives. It asks to what extent and how young people growing up in spaces characterized by networks, values and social relationships that are indicative of bonding social capital, can straddle boundaries and access and generate bridging social capital.

A study of transitions

This paper draws on data collected in Northern Ireland as part of a qualitative longitudinal study of young people growing up in five very different locations across the UK. The *Inventing Adulthoods*[1] study has followed a group of about 100 young people (aged 11–17 at the start) over more than ten years from 1996, with up to six interviews with each participant.[2] The participants were drawn from five socio-economically contrasting sites across the UK including Northern Ireland, where the group varied by social class and community/ethno-religious/cultural identification. The methods included a questionnaire, focus groups, lifelines, and memory books (a form of diary), but the main method was repeated biographical interviews.[3] We adopted a longitudinal, qualitative, biographical approach to examine the micro-processes that contribute to the diverse biographical projects in which young people engage, walking alongside them through time (Du Bois-Reymond 1998; Ball, Maguire and Macrae 2000; McLeod 2000; Neale 2002; Thomson et al. 2002). Young people are faced with the task of 'inventing adulthood' because material and social conditions have shifted significantly in the course of a generation, perhaps particularly so in Northern Ireland. By listening to their narratives of self, developing and changing over time (Chamberlayne, Bornat and Wengraf 2000; Miller 2000; Plummer 2001), we have tried to gain insight into the relationship between the unique life (biography), the context within which it is lived (structural dimensions), and the processes of which it is part (for example, history, social change, social mobility) (Coles 1995, 2000; Du Bois-Reymond and Lopez Blasco 2003; MacDonald et al. 2005; Henderson et al. 2007).

The political, religious and cultural divisions in Northern Ireland run deeply through its history, revealing the play of power in their production and perpetuation. Whilst broad global, historical and social processes might potentially have led in the direction of change in this situation in the mid-twentieth century, a phase of open hostility and violent conflict in the early 1970s stopped this process in its tracks, preserving, enhancing and entrenching the ethno-religious-political divide characterized as sectarian, Protestant and Catholic (Brewer 1998; Brewer and Higgins 1999). The long and painful peace process that has followed 'the Troubles' itself attests to the tenacity of the division, which plays a significant part in the lived lives and biographical narratives of the young people in our study.

Academics and commentators have invested in the complex and often contradictory relationships between politics, nationalism, ethnicity, religion, sectarianism and territoriality in describing and theorizing the situation in Northern Ireland (Anderson and Shuttleworth 1998). Sectarianism is the core for Smyth and Moore (1996), and McVeigh (1998) conceptualizes the division in ethnic terms, drawing a link between ethnicity, sectarianism and racism. Throughout a long history, outward migration has been characteristic of Ireland, north and south. But as the economy expanded post-ceasefire, and work opportunities increased, inward migration brought many from Eastern Europe and beyond to work in the country (Jarman 2005). This inward migration has added to the increasing cultural diversity and ethnic pluralism of Northern Ireland. It has also highlighted a level of bigotry and racism that many would argue always existed but was masked by sectarianism (Mussano 2004) and bolstered by state policies (Lentin and McVeigh 2006). The presence of overt and institutional racism (Connolly 2002) and the documented rise in the number of racist attacks and incidents of harassment in Northern Ireland (Jarman 2003; Jarman and Monaghan 2003) since the ceasefires of the 1990s have led some commentators to suggest that racism is the new sectarianism. A more pragmatic view taken by McVeigh and Rolston (2007) suggests that sectarianism is still very much a part of Northern Irish society and that racism is merely the other side of that coin.

We have documented some of the changes in the lives of young people that have been enabled by the peace process in terms of crossing the lines of division (McGrellis 2005a). These relate particularly to youth and club culture, and the possibilities of physically moving into the spaces of 'the other' through work or leisure activities, leading on occasion to mixed relationships (Caballero, Edwards and Smith 2008). But this is very far, for example, from the 'convivial culture' that Gilroy (2004) identifies and envisages as the way forward for living with ethnic diversity and difference in metropolitan centres in the UK. Gilroy's convivial culture is related to youth lifestyles, the interactions that make multiculture part of everyday life in Britain's urban areas, and emancipatory interruptions that can open spaces for change, but the approach is not without criticism.

The *Inventing Adulthoods* project began in 1996 and data generation coincided with significant developments and crises in the 'peace process'. Paramilitary ceasefires called in 1994 had collapsed prior to the first wave of data collection (1996). The Good Friday/Belfast Agreement in 1998 heralded the setting up of a historic devolved government body in 1999, a structure that was suspended in 2002 and only reinstated again in 2007. Uncertainty, expectation, fear and instability characterized the political landscape for much of the time during which the research was carried out. Sectarian violence continued, communities remained defensive and narratives of change and optimism were given cautious welcome, and at times frustrated rebuff. Over the years, young people in the study engaged with the political developments and discourse to a greater or lesser extent. In the early interviews (1997 to 1999), discussions on the 'peace process', community differences, sectarian violence, and shared spaces were animated, at times heated, and drew on young people's own lived experience and the historical experience of their families and communities. Subsequent interviews, however, suggested that participants had largely disengaged from politics, and from whatever was happening (or not happening) in the corridors of Stormont and Westminster. The political changes and developments nonetheless contributed to their biographical narratives of community, affiliation, identity and perceived opportunity. They responded to opportunities and challenges that came with the changing political landscape in ways that either reflected new optimism and confidence or enduring fear and suspicion.

Theoretical starting points

We have drawn on the work of the Families and Social Capital Research Group in our use of the concept of social capital (www.lsbu.ac.uk/families). Their definition of the concept derives from the main social capital theorists and suggests that social capital consists of 'the values people hold and the resources that they can access, which both result in and are the result of collective and socially negotiated ties and relationships'. We have also drawn on Putnam, who stresses 'features of social organisation, such as networks, norms and trust that facilitate action and co-operation for mutual benefit' (1993, p. 35), and in particular his elaborations of the concept as incorporating bonding and bridging social capital. Bonding social capital tends to be inward-looking and to reinforce exclusive identities and homogeneous groups; bridging social capital involves outward-looking connections across diverse social cleavages. It has been argued that bonding social capital enables people to 'get by', whilst bridging social capital enables them to 'get on'. In common with others (e.g. Reynolds 2006) our findings enable us to both critique and elaborate these concepts. The longitudinal biographical approach brings to light both complex interactional processes involving layers of bonding and bridging that permeate families and communities, and the agency of young people in deploying social capital to access resources in support of their biographical projects. The three case studies used in this article (Adrian, Cynthia and Cheryl) exemplify these complex processes.

Boundaried spaces: territory and mobility

Within each of the case studies we also observe the extent to which young people's biographies are influenced by their relationship to space and territory. This theme is more fully explored in McGrellis (2005b) but considered here in the context of mobility and how mobility shapes and influences the type and nature of social capital available to young people on their transitional journeys. Geographical and social mobility is a major theme running throughout the Northern Ireland dataset. Young people repeatedly talked about their aspirations to leave Northern Ireland, for work, education or travel. Recent data from the study confirm that over 50 per cent did in fact leave the province for one or other of these reasons.

Mobility linked to educational, occupational and lifestyle or leisure choices is a key part of young people's transitions to adulthood (Thomson and Taylor 2005; Henderson et al. 2007). Geographical mobility is a feature of life for many within Northern Ireland, as it was for the third-level students who took part in David Cairns's study (2008), many of whom subscribed to the view that they needed to get out in order to get on. These findings are echoed in a study by Smyth and colleagues (2004), and Adrian's experience in England (see later) led him to the same conclusion. Many of the young people in a study by Ewart and colleagues (2004) gave political disillusionment as a reason why they would consider leaving Northern Ireland, a sentiment also expressed by the young people in this study.

Not all major journeys involve great distances. Crossing territorial boundaries, as Cheryl did, and negotiating unfamiliar spaces continues to be an issue for young people, despite over a decade of 'peace'. The 'Troubles' accentuated differences between Catholic and Protestant communities and have contributed to increased segregation through widespread population shifts. In a spirit of confidence and optimism immediately following the paramilitary ceasefire in 1994, over 3,000 people moved into areas dominated by the other community; between 1996 and 2002 over 6,000 retreated to segregated housing areas (Brown 2002). Residential segregation has been a feature of life in Northern Ireland since before the 'Troubles', but from the beginning of that period ongoing movement and displacement have contributed to a situation where up to 40 per cent of the total population live in communities divided along ethno-sectarian lines (Hughes et al. 2007). Fear and mistrust continue to keep communities apart, frustrating overall social and economic development (Shirlow 2000; Roche 2008).

Given the deep fear and mistrust that has existed in Northern Ireland over the past few decades, progress on community relations is likely to be a slow process (Heaney 1990; Finlay 1999). Studies that record this process over time give a valuable insight into change in attitudes and behaviour and the factors that facilitate such changes. The data from a longitudinal study (Hewstone et al. 2008) of 'direct' and 'indirect' community contact in mixed and segregated areas in Belfast suggest that extended contact via friends and family members over time was more effective on a range of measures than contact via work colleagues or neighbours. In addition the study found that those living in mixed areas were more willing to engage in contact and did not feel as threatened or as distant from the 'outgroup'.

In a study by Madeleine Leonard (2009), teenagers living in 'one of the most contested areas of Northern Ireland' were in principle open to the idea of cross-community marriages, but identified a range of practical dilemmas that might stop them marrying outside their community. Despite this, Leonard suggests that these teenagers are more receptive towards the idea of mixed marriages than perhaps their parents would be, and welcomes this as progress. An increased preference for mixed religion neighbourhoods (from 50 per cent in 2003 to 62 per cent in 2007) among young people who completed the Young Life and Times survey could also be regarded as progress (Schubotz and Devine 2008). A determination to create more mixed community housing is part of Northern Ireland's New Housing Agenda 2008, and follows the principles of the Shared Future Document, which sets out policy and action for government and civil society to address sectarianism and racism at all levels, and improve community relations across Northern Ireland (Community Relations Unit 2005).

Social capital in Northern Ireland

Successful social and political transition in Northern Ireland depends on the sharing of spaces and resources, on building bridges and making links and connections – on generating 'bridging social capital'. Morrow (2006) emphasizes the need for such work in his paper on sustainable development in Northern Ireland, arguing that networks and trust need to be fostered at all levels, including, and most particularly, at a policy level. However, as Leonard (2004) found out in her study of social capital in West Belfast, moving from 'bonding' to 'bridging' in politically contentious societies is not straightforward and can have 'an unequal effect within those communities most affected by the wider political system'. Leonard argues that communities such as those she studied in West Belfast, which would traditionally be regarded as displaying strong bonding social capital, are in themselves not homogeneous, and that the inequalities that exist already within such communities can be emphasized in the transition to bridging capital in terms of 'unequal benefits'. That said, it is recognized that communities bonded closely together as much for political as social reasons during the conflict, and so while it could be argued that the peace process has created a new environment where 'bridging' social capital can be more easily generated, it is not necessarily a straightforward transition, nor one that brings equal benefits to all.

The biographical stories of participants in the *Inventing Adulthoods* study reveal the interplay between social structures and the individual agency that young people exercise on their transitional journeys. Observing the way that they create or access social capital, in changing and challenging environments and at critical moments, allows us to consider how processes of social reproduction, detraditionalization and globalization are at work within their lives. The use of case studies throws light on the importance of social capital in the often complex trajectories that can emerge from the intersection of ethnicity, community, gender and religion, and on the relationship between bonding and bridging capital. We see from the case studies below that some aspects of bonding social capital actually enable individuals to move on and beyond what could be regarded as its more restrictive and dark side. Adrian's story is an example of this. The type of social capital that works to keep young people who grow up in a divided society safe within their own confessional areas is positive in its protective nature but can be damaging for long-term broader community relations and growth. Cheryl's journey across community boundaries was significant at a personal level but limited in its bridging capacity, lacking as it did the trust and sustained backing of her community of influence. Bridging social capital is not easily available in tightly knit and closed sectarian communities. However, for Cynthia, and indeed Adrian, geographical mobility in itself provided them with distance and perspective, and the ability to observe the effects of sectarianism and ethnic division rather than merely absorb them. Adrian's experience in some way challenges Putnam's analysis of bonding social capital as inward-looking, reinforcing exclusive identities and restrictive in terms of geographical or social mobility. As we see below, it was this type of social capital that allowed Adrian to progress beyond the confines of his community.

Adrian

Adrian is a young man whose transition to adulthood was marked by an event that propelled him into an unknown world where the processes of social capital worked to ensure his personal safety and allowed him to experience life beyond his local community, to observe its limitations and to question what he himself subscribed to as normal. His case study shows how a young man reconstructs his own identity through a process of physical and social mobility. It illustrates the interplay between bonding and bridging social capital and how these can operate to good effect within a diasporic community. Adrian's case study suggests that the experience of living within a wider multi-ethnic community outside Northern Ireland both masks and emphasizes ethnic boundaries that are drawn along religious and sectarian lines within it. The Protestants he meets and works with in England are part of the Irish diaspora, all 'Paddys', but Adrian also includes them among the more wide-ranging ethnic groups he has come into contact with since leaving Northern Ireland, now for him a part of everyday life, presaging, perhaps, convivial ethnicities? Extending the link between his two worlds, Adrian brings one of his Northern Irish Protestant friends to his parental home for a social visit – as remarkable to him in the telling as the stories of living among his Asian and Muslim neighbours.

Growing up in a respectable working-class nationalist area Adrian enjoyed the security and sense of belonging that came from being part of a large and extended family. The repercussions of a contested but violent incident saw Adrian 'expelled' by paramilitaries within hours from this tight-knit and secure environment. Paramilitaries exercised their authority to police the community in which he lived – an authority that was accorded to such groups as a result of the lack of trust in official bodies – a situation that for some represented the dark side of bonding social capital. While Adrian was cleared by the courts of any wrongdoing he was nonetheless 'sentenced' to a year in exile.

Before this critical moment (Thomson et al. 2002) in his life, Adrian had just left school, aged 16, and taken up a trade apprenticeship. His social life involved hanging out with friends locally. His political views were influenced by the nationalist/republican tradition of the community in which he lived. He had no real contact with people of a different ethnicity, religion or political persuasion, and, as he said, had no desire to leave his local community:

'Between my family and my friends, they are the two things I never ever wanted to leave.' (age 18, 1999)

He shared with his friends a particular aversion to any thought of travel to or connection with England. It is ironic therefore that his expulsion led him to England and to a life where he slowly extended his social world and his economic capacity, and developed a sense of himself beyond but very much connected to and informed by his family and community.

The move to England saw him draw extensively on family and community networks there – some of whom were initially strangers to him. Providing key forms of social capital, they ensured that he was cared for physically, socially and emotionally, that he completed his education and training, and that he was in a better position at the end of that year to generate his own social and economic capital.

Adrian developed friendships and contacts with people from different cultural backgrounds from his own – which he admits made him 'open up a bit'. He maintained close contact with his family and some friends at home. As he grew in confidence he encouraged friends and siblings to follow his path out of Northern Ireland – a place he came to regard as 'small' and lacking in opportunity.

While making contact and friends with people from various ethnic and cultural backgrounds, Adrian drew strongly on Irish networks in England. He capitalized on his ethnicity as a resource to secure work and build a reputation for himself in a place that was initially alien and frightening to him. On the strength of the resources and support he received from family in England, he moved to other parts of the country, but largely lived and worked within the Irish diaspora – drawing on the social networks and economic capital of this group. He maintained that being Irish was an asset in acquiring work, and was prepared to capitalize on it as such:

'with us being Irish too we were way at the top of the list like with the agencies, so (we were) turning down work every day' (age 23, 2004)

His term of expulsion over and his name cleared, Adrian was able to return home, which he did, but only for visits. The critical moment in his life challenged his prejudices and values and put him on a path that depended initially on 'bonding social capital' made available to him by close family networks and satellites. Bolstered by this support, he confidently bridged into a bigger social space, a space which included many different ethnic groups and cultures (including, as he observed, Protestants), but a space nonetheless framed by a strong sense of his ethnicity and identity.

'They just know me as Paddy, they all call me Paddy, all the Muslims and that that I know and Asians and that. They're all sound like, I get on well with them all.' (age 23, 2004)

The social capital that Adrian was able to draw on and subsequently generate for himself ensured a positive transitional step and outcome for him. It could be argued that the type of social capital Adrian used to make this successful transition remained within the realm of bonding capital, drawing largely as he did on his own ethnic heritage and extended family links. He, like the young people in Reynolds's study (2006), drew heavily on resources that were largely accessible on the basis of his ethnicity and were fostered within diasporic communities that formed primarily around ethnic identity. Adrian depended on these networks and resources at a time when he was especially vulnerable. He, in turn, however, became a conduit for the successful transmission of social capital within his own family, sponsoring, as he did, his younger brothers in their journeys out of Northern Ireland and the more limited economic opportunities it offered them.

The question is to what extent Adrian's journey represents a transition from bonding to bridging social capital. In Putnam's analysis, bridging social capital generates positive outcomes for the community. In this instance, it could be argued, the benefits were felt largely by Adrian's immediate family of origin and his new diasporic community – a fluid and ever changing community of reference. He, however, continued to widen his social, cultural and economic horizons through travel abroad and various work initiatives. A concerted and combined response from a close-knit diasporic community at a critical moment in his life facilitated a successful transition into adulthood. Adrian was equipped with the tools and working blocks to begin to generate his own social capital in a space beyond his immediate community but remaining very much connected to it.

We will now consider the processes involved for a young woman whose strong investment in her identity and ethnicity created barriers for her and who, unlike Adrian, found it more difficult to capitalize on this as a resource.

Cynthia

Cynthia is a young Scottish woman who came to live in Northern Ireland with her family when she was 11 years old. Her story illustrates difficulties and tensions that can exist for young people as they attempt to reconcile the contradictions of community, place, politics, ethnicity and religion. It also illustrates how a strong investment in ethnic identity can create barriers and frustrate attempts to tap into localized networks and social capital. Her case study shows how attempts to draw on ethnicity as social capital are complicated and frustrated by social structures and processes that are framed by sectarianism. Cynthia's sense of belonging was disrupted when her family moved from Scotland to Northern Ireland. The move constituted a critical moment in her life, removing her from extended family and friends and all that was familiar to her up until that point. Relocation to Northern Ireland undermined her connection to place, but emphasized aspects of her identity that were defined by her gender, culture, religion and politics. The interplay between these and the way in which they were both acted out and perceived in her new surroundings illustrate the complex processes involved for young people in constructing and maintaining their own sense of self in conflicted spaces.

> '"are you a nationalist or are you a loyalist?" but I would say "I'm a Scottish nationalist" and automatically I think people at work think I'm a Catholic and I goes "no I'm not" and they go "Oh of course you are", and I goes but "no I'm not, you could be a nationalist but that's nothing to do with me and nothing to do with religion". [. . .] like I said before the minute I arrived here it was such a culture shock I had never seen anybody as like a Protestant or anything like that I just seen everybody as my friends who I walked to school with, who ever you are they've a name not the religion.' (age 18, 2003)

While sectarianism also exists in some parts of Scotland it had no everyday impact on Cynthia.

Despite having family connections in Northern Ireland, Cynthia felt very much an outsider when she moved there. Up until that point, she had lived a life where space, identity and culture were, in her experience, uncontested, and her sense of identity and belonging was overwhelmingly confirmed. On moving, this all changed. Her family initially moved to a mixed estate (Catholics and a small number of Protestants), which Cynthia described as 'a scary environment'. They were forced to align themselves with one or other community and so relocated to a 'purely Protestant area' which to Cynthia felt much safer and 'more protected'. The strong localized bonding within this community gave her and her family a sense of security. She enrolled in a local secondary school attended on the whole by young people from the Protestant community. Although she was brought up as a Protestant, it was not, she argued, a significant part of her identity. However, in her new living environment, religion became a more defining element and Cynthia found herself having to defend aspects of her identity that had previously gone unquestioned. She was forced to unpack the significance and interrelationship between religion, politics, nationality and culture in her own life and to understand how these were mediated in the lives of those in the community of which she was now a part. Football was a major part of Cynthia's cultural life and her support for Rangers football club was as much a family and historical tradition as it was an expression of her nationality. Her bedroom was a shrine to Scotland and to Rangers:

'my main thing is like my football, that's me [. . .] my room is I've got a big, I drew a big mural of RFC. You know the actual emblem, logo, I put, I drew it up on my wall and painted it and I've got Scotland [. . .] on my roof and then I've got wee mini Scotlands all round and a big Scotland poster as well.' (age 15, 2000)

In Northern Ireland (as in Scotland) support for Rangers football club can be an expression of Protestantism and in some cases of a loyalist tradition, and it has also been used as a front for sectarianism. While joining a local Rangers football supporters club could have possibly fostered a sense of social inclusion for Cynthia, she resisted on the basis that her support was more about family tradition and inheritance and less about religion. The meaning Cynthia attached to her support for Rangers differed from what she saw as the collective norm, further emphasizing her difference and sense of alienation.

'If I do wake up in the morning and throw on my Rangers top it's not because I'm a Protestant and that's the only reason I support Rangers, it's because my whole family throughout the whole entire history has supported Rangers and I've just kind of inherited that.' (age 18, 2003)

Cynthia was initially able to draw on her difference and her ethnicity as resources – she commanded attention and friendships in her new school as the 'loud Scottish girl' and made friends on the strength of her difference. She used her difference in an effort to resist being categorized according to labels that already existed. She was unable, however, to sustain this and found that her difference was as easily used to exclude her as it was to include. Unable to find a foothold in her new place of residence, Cynthia also found, to her dismay, that she was simultaneously losing her connection to her Scottish homeland, and sadly reflected that her sense of belonging and identity was somewhere in the sea between Scotland and Ireland.

Throughout her early interviews Cynthia voiced her intention to return to Scotland at her earliest opportunity. As she got older, this dream wavered and she increasingly directed energy into the expanding youth and club culture. Being part of this space enabled her to make the sorts of connections and networks that facilitated confidence and belonging, something that she was unable to develop, or prevented from developing, in the early years following her move to Northern Ireland.

Cheryl

Cheryl's story casts a light on the early tentative journeys that some young people made post-ceasefire to engage with a growing night-time youth culture and to create and capitalize on spaces that were less differentiating and divisive than those they came from. The resources needed and risks taken in order to make such moves, and also to be part of a globalized youth consumer market, were highly significant for young people like Cheryl. Mobility at the physical and social level could be seen as undermining or challenging the supportive but restrictive form of bonding social capital that single-identity communities like hers depend on.

When we first met Cheryl at the age of 15 she was firmly located within her local working-class Protestant community. The estate in which she grew up was 'close-knit' in the sense that 'everyone looks out for each other', and it was a place that portrayed a defended and united identity, made visible to the outsider by the flying of loyalist and union flags and painted kerbstones. As outlined elsewhere (McGrellis 2005a, 2005b), it was generally young men who took on responsibility as the guardians and custodians of such spaces.

Cheryl recognized and subscribed to the exclusionary rules that governed the spaces she lived and socialized in. Her community could be described as insular and typical of a community dependent on and supported by bonding social capital. At our first meeting Cheryl was of the firm view that segregated communities were a good and necessary thing. Her uncle had been killed during the Troubles and she used this as a justification for her strong views against any form of community integration, or personal contact with Catholics:

'No I think we should be kept apart. [...] My uncle was killed and I think it's just really they should be completely kept apart. [...] My parents would kill me if I ever went out with a Catholic.' (age 15, 1998)

In our early meetings Cheryl drew heavily on her local and family community for social and economic capital, and for confirmation of her sense of who she was in terms of ethnic and national identity. Cheryl grew in confidence as she established greater independence from her parents, through local part-time work, a steady relationship with a local lad, and engagement in a cross-community (single-identity) project. All of these activities slowly introduced her to other spaces and people and both confirmed and challenged her sense of belonging and community at both the localized and the wider community level. Through part-time work in a high street store she became friendly with a young Catholic woman. This represented the first real and naturally occurring contact Cheryl had with someone from the Catholic community. It challenged her perceptions and gave her a taste of the possibilities that lay beyond the space she traditionally committed to.

Leaving school at 17 was the trigger for Cheryl to leave home – for the first time. She secured a full-time job in her wider local area, got lodgings in the same estate as her parental home, but most significantly began to socialize in different and more 'risky' circles. These spaces were risky only in the sense that they fell beyond the protective net of her own local community, and the young men who 'guarded' her local territory. Having split from her first long-term boyfriend Cheryl enjoyed the freedom to date and engage in short-term romances in new social spaces, the most significant of these romances being with a young Catholic man:

'My biggest thing of the year is that I went with a Catholic. For four months. [...] I never thought that I could ever get on with [Catholic] people [...] and none of them [young men] ever knew I was going with him. They thought we were friends. My girlfriends knew he was a Catholic but the fellas just sort of thought he was a fella from [...] on down the country. Whenever we finished it did come out that he was Catholic, [...] and they did give me a hard time.' (age 18, 2001)

Cheryl's journeys beyond her local area energized her and encouraged her to take risks in order to access a different and wider pool of financial and social resources. She also persuaded some of her female friends to join her, adding strength, security and increased sustainability to this pursuit. These journeys, though not significant in mileage or culture, nonetheless represented first opportunities to foster and access networks of a kind that had the potential to translate into bridging social capital.

Going beyond the close and bonded ties of localized communities enables young people like Cheryl to challenge the restrictive transmission of bonding social capital that is solely funnelled along ethnic tracks. The strategic use of networks for leisure and economic gain is one way that young people in this study created and seized opportunities for real linking and bridging. These advances, while positive, remain fragile and tentative, as without structural support and the endorsement of significant players within the community, most notably young men, they are limited in terms of overall community development.

Cheryl:	'Well actually we're plucking up the courage to move over the town. The fellas won't go over, but the girls [...] we're going to head there [...] so we're organizing quite a lot of girls nights.
Interviewer:	So when you say you're plucking up the courage – is that the whole business of crossing over –
Cheryl:	Aye, going over the town. None of the fellas will, but I don't think the girls are not minding as much now.

(age 18, 2001)

Conclusion

These young people's transitions to adulthood have taken place against significant developments in Northern Ireland where continuities of traditional ethnic and community values and identities have been disrupted by social, political and economic change. From different starting points and embedded in lives characterized by close communities and bonding social capital, they have each moved into different territories. Two were able to move from bonding to bridging social capital and to judiciously combine them in the route to broader horizons. The other was displaced, moving from one close-knit community to another, and her efforts to maintain connection with one frustrated her sense of belonging and acceptance in the other, and, as she commented herself, left her feeling somewhere at sea between the two places.

Afloat in the sea is perhaps the most vulnerable place to be, a place where neither the anchor of bonding social capital nor the lifebelt of bridging capital are readily available for use. As the *Inventing Adulthoods* study has shown, young people do find themselves afloat, like Cynthia, at various times in their lives. The availability of trusted networks, contacts and resources at such times can make the difference in terms of successful transitions and the ability to overcome difficult life events. As outlined in this paper, the relationship between bonding and bridging social capital is not clear-cut and the young people in this study drew on, created, and benefited from both at various points in their biographical trajectories. For successful transitions, especially in the face of critical life events, the ability to access resources and networks within a closely bonded, or ethnically defined, community is by these accounts important and has implications for the way in which young people can and do move beyond their communities of reference.

Trust, communication, confidence and freedom of movement were all central to the young people's transitional journeys and their ability to access and build social capital at critical moments. These same elements are essential to community development across Northern Ireland, and to the success of *its* transitional journey. Part of this journey requires it to move from a society that is more characterized by bonding social capital to one that benefits from bridging capital. It is imperative that, as Morrow (2006) argues, the building blocks for creating real and sustainable networks and trust between communities are established at the public policy level, and across all sectors and structures of society. The principles enshrined within the 'Shared Future' document (Community Relations Unit 2005) support this vision for development. Making the vision a reality is the responsibility of all, but needs to be driven by government.

Acknowledgements

The author wishes to acknowledge Professor Janet Holland's contribution to the revised version of this paper, and the constructive comments of three referees on an earlier draft.

Notes

1. The core team of researchers on the Inventing Adulthoods project are Sheila Henderson, Janet Holland, Sheena McGrellis, Sue Sharpe and Rachel Thomson.
2. Funded throughout by the UK Economic and Social Research Council on a series of programmes of research (L129251020, L134251008, M570255001), Inventing Adulthoods (www.lsbu.ac.uk/inventingadulthoods) is now in archiving and longitudinal analysis mode as a part of *Timescapes: Changing Relationships and Identities through the Life Course* (www.timescapes.leeds.ac.uk; RES-347-25-0003). London South Bank University also provided support.
3. The methods of data collection are described in detail on the project website (http://www.lsbu.ac.uk/inventingadulthoods).

References

ANDERSON, JAMES and SHUTTLEWORTH, IAN 1998 'Sectarianism demography and political development in Northern Ireland', *Political Geography*, vol. 17, no. 2, pp. 187–208
BALL, STEPHEN, MAGUIRE, MEG and MACRAE, SHEILA 2000 *Choice, Pathways and Transitions Post-16*, London: Routledge
BREWER, JOHN D. 1998 *Anti-Catholicism in Northern Ireland 1600–1998: The Mote and the Beam*, London: Macmillan
BREWER, JOHN D. and HIGGINS, GARETH I. 1999 'Understanding anti-Catholicism in Northern Ireland', *Sociology*, vol. 33, no. 2, pp. 235–55
BROWN, PAUL 2002 'Peace but no love as Northern Ireland divide grows ever wider', *Guardian*, 4 January, http://www.guardian.co.uk/Archive/Article/0,4273,4328995,00.html
CABALLERO, CHAMION, EDWARDS, ROSALIND and SMITH, DARREN 2008 'Cultures of mixing: understanding partnerships across ethnicity', *Twenty-First Century Society: Journal of the Academy of Social Sciences*, vol. 3, no. 1, pp. 49–63
CAIRNS, DAVID 2008 'Moving in transition: Northern Ireland youth and geographical mobility', *Young*, vol. 16, no. 3, pp. 227–49
CHAMBERLAYNE, PRUE, BORNAT, JOANNA and WENGRAF, TOM (eds) 2000 *The Turn to Biographical Methods in Social Science. Comparative Issues and Examples*, London: Routledge
COLES, BOB 1995 *Youth and Social Policy: Youth Citizenship and Young Careers*, London: UCL Press
——— 2000 *Joined Up Youth Research, Policy and Practice: An Agenda for Change?* Leicester: Youth Work Press
COMMUNITY RELATIONS UNIT (2005) *A Shared Future: Policy and Strategic Framework for Good Relations in Northern Ireland*, Belfast: Community Relations Unit, Office of the First Minister and Deputy First Minister, www.asharedfutureni.gov.uk
CONNOLLY, PAUL 2002 'Race and racism in Northern Ireland: a review of the research evidence', Belfast: OFMDFM Research Branch
DU BOIS-REYMOND, MANUELA 1998 "I don't want to commit myself yet": young people's life concepts, *Journal of Youth Studies*, vol. 1, pp. 63–79
DU BOIS-REYMOND, MANUELA and LOPEZ BLASCO, ANDREU 2003 'Yo-yo transitions and misleading trajectories: towards integrated transition policies for young adults in Europe', in Andreu Lopez Blasco, W. McNeish, and A. Walther (eds), *Young People and Contradictions of Inclusion: Towards Integrated Transition Policies in Europe*, Bristol: Policy Press
EWART, SHIRLEY *et al.* 2004 *Voices Behind the Statistics: Young People's Views of Sectarianism in Northern Ireland*, Research Report, Northern Ireland Young Life and Times and National Children's Bureau, Belfast
FINLAY, ANDREW 1999 '"Whatever you say say nothing": an ethnographic encounter in Northern Ireland and its sequel', *Sociological Research Online*, vol. 4, no. 3, http://www.socresonline.org.uk/socresonline/4/3/finlay.html
GILROY, PAUL 2004 *After Empire: Melancholia or Convivial Culture?*, London: Routledge
HEANEY, SEAMUS 1990 *New Selected Poems 1966–1987*, London: Faber and Faber
HENDERSON, SHEILA, *et al.* 2007 *Inventing Adulthoods: A Biographical Approach to Youth Transitions*, London: Sage and Open University
HEWSTONE, MILES *et al.* 2008 'Can contact promote better relations? Evidence from mixed and segregated areas of Belfast', Belfast: Office of the First Minister and Deputy First Minister, http://www.ofmdfmni.gov.uk/
HUGHES, JOANNE, *et al.* 2007 'Segregation in Northern Ireland', *Policy Studies*, vol. 28, no. 1, pp. 33–53
JARMAN, NEIL 2003 'Victims and perpetrators, racism and young people in Northern Ireland', *Child Care in Practice*, vol. 9, no. 2, pp. 129–39

——— 2005 *Changing Patterns and Future Planning. Migration and Northern Ireland*, Working Paper No. 1, Belfast: Institute for Conflict Research

JARMAN, NEIL and MONAGHAN, RACHEL 2003 *Racist Harassment in Northern Ireland*, commissioned for the Office of the First and Deputy First Minister, Belfast: Institute for Conflict Research

LENTIN, RONIT and MCVEIGH, ROBBIE 2006 *After Optimism? Racism and Globalisation*, Dublin: Metro Eireann Publications

LEONARD, MADELEINE 2004 'Bonding and bridging social capital: reflections from Belfast', *Sociology*, vol. 38, no. 5, pp. 927–44

——— 2009 '"It's better to stick to your own kind": teenagers' views on cross-community marriages in Northern Ireland', *Journal of Ethnic and Migration Studies*, vol. 35, no. 1, pp. 97–113

MACDONALD, ROBERT, *et al.* 2005 'Growing up in poor neighbourhoods: the significance of class and place in the extended transitions of "socially excluded" young adults', *Sociology*, vol. 39, no. 5, pp. 873–91

MCGRELLIS, SHEENA 2005a 'Pushing the boundaries in Northern Ireland: young people, violence and sectarianism', *Contemporary Politics*, vol. 11, no. 1, pp. 53–71

——— 2005b 'Pure and bitter spaces: gender, identity and territory in Northern Irish youth transitions', *Gender and Education*, vol. 17, no. 5, pp. 515–29

MCLEOD, JULIE 2000 'Subjectivity and schooling in a longitudinal study of secondary students', *British Journal of Sociology of Education*, vol. 21, pp. 502–21

MCVEIGH, ROBBIE 1998 'Is sectarianism racism? The implications of sectarian division for multi-ethnicity in Ireland', paper presented at 'The Expanding Nation towards a Multi-Ethnic Ireland' conference, Trinity College Dublin

MCVEIGH, ROBBIE and ROLSTON, BILL 2007 'From Good Friday to Good Relations: sectarianism, racism and the Northern Ireland state', *Race and Class*, vol. 48, no. 4, pp. 1–23

MILLER, ROBERT 2000 *Researching Life Stories and Family Histories*, London: Sage

MORROW, DUNCAN 2006 'Sustainability in a divided society – applying social capital theory to Northern Ireland', *Shared Space*, issue 2, May, pp. 63–80

MUSSANO, SILVIA 2004 'Citizenship education policies in Northern Ireland and the recognition of ethnic and racial diversity in the wake of new immigration', *Migration Letters*, vol. 1, no. 1, pp. 2–10

NEALE, BREN 2002 'Dialogues with children: children, divorce and citizenship', *Childhood*, vol. 9, no. 4, pp. 455–75

PLUMMER, KEN 2001 *Documents of Life 2: A Critical Invitation to Humanism*, London: Sage

PUTNAM, ROBERT D. 1993 *Making Democracy Work: Civic Traditions in Modern Italy*, Princeton: Princeton University Press

REYNOLDS, TRACEY 2006 'Bonding social capital within the Caribbean family and community', *Journal of Community, Work and Family*, vol. 9, no. 3, pp. 273–90

ROCHE, ROSELLEN 2008 'Facts, fears and feelings project', Queens University Belfast, http://www.innovations-report.com/html/reports/social_sciences/report-113060.html

SCHUBOTZ, DIRK and DEVINE, PAULA (eds) 2008 *Young People in Post-Conflict Northern Ireland: The Past Cannot Be Changed But the Future Can Be Developed*, Dorset: Russell House Publishing

SHIRLOW, PETER (2000) *Fear, Mobility and Living in the Ardoyne and Upper Ardoyne Communities*, report by Mapping the Spaces of Fear Research Team, University of Ulster Coleraine

SMYTH, MARIE and MOORE, RUTH 1996 *'Researching Sectarianism'. Five Conference Papers on Aspects of Segregation and Sectarian Division*, Derry/Londonderry: Templegrove Action Research Ltd

SMYTH, MARIE, *et al.* 2004 *The Impact of Political Conflict in Northern Ireland: A Report on the Community Conflict Impact on Children Study*, Belfast: Institute for Conflict Research

THOMSON, RACHEL and TAYLOR, REBECCA 2005 'Between cosmopolitanism and the locals: mobility as a resource in the transition to adulthood', *Young*, vol. 13, no. 4, pp. 327–42
THOMSON, RACHEL, *et al.* 2002 'Critical moments: choice, chance and opportunity in young people's narratives of transition to adulthood', *Sociology*, vol. 36, no. 2, pp. 335–54

Social networks and identity negotiations of religious minority youth in diverse social contexts

Arniika Kuusisto

Abstract

This study is looking at how youth growing up in families affiliated with a religious minority negotiate their religious values and social identity in the social contexts of minority and majority. Although these youth belong to the ethnic majority in Finland, the religious and lifestyle values of their home and religious community differ from the Lutheran mainstream, which causes discrepancies between the values of their socialization background and those of their peer group. The negotiations of values and identities are here examined through two case examples of the teenagers' interview data. These examples illustrate the varied strategies for negotiation, positive versus negative experiences on the acquired negotiation outcomes, as well as the diversity within a minority community and the different ways of being a member of a religious minority.

Introduction

This study is looking at how religious minority youth, Finnish Seventh-day Adventist (hereafter referred to as Adventist) teenagers, negotiate their religious values and social identity, by examining the influence of the social contexts of minority and majority on these negotiations and on the youths' social networks. The everyday value negotiations and the strategies for solving these reflect, through similarity and difference, the experienced belongings to the minority on one hand and the majority on the other (e.g. Joseph [2006]).

Thereby, these processes contribute to their *belonging* – as emotional attachment, or feeling 'at home' (Yuval-Davis 2006, p. 199) – and thereby to their social identity.

There's a lack of data on ethnicity and religious communities (Modood 2005, p. 3); furthermore, in multicultural analyses, religious minorities within the ethnic majority are often disregarded. This is regrettable, since the increasing pluralism in Western societies sets new demands on policies and institutions, thus up-to-date understanding of a range of minorities is essential to a comprehensive view. Identity construction is particularly timely in youth (Kroger 2004, p. 7), when identity work is often very much in process (Helve 2002, p. 222). The identity negotiations of religious minority youth in diverse social settings can parallel those of ethnic minority youth. Thus, the present research design and findings are relevant from the perspective of research on ethnicity; critical race studies and whiteness studies (Frankenberg 1993; Jay 2007) in particular.

In her book on the social construction of whiteness, Ruth Frankenberg (1993, p. 1) sees whiteness as (1) location, (2) standpoint, and (3) in reference to a set of particular cultural practices. Although 'whites' are often seen to hold a race privilege (Frankenberg 1993, p. 1), the variation in, for example, economical, political and religious situations creates different power positions – either actual or perceived – also for the groups and individuals within such ethnic groups. These positions are fluid, and depend on both the particular subject matter, its personal relevance to the individual and her value system, and the specific context. Perhaps the fluidity is even more noteworthy among the same ethnic group when the minority identity can be concealed and thereby the negotiations privatized, as in the case of the presently studied youth, most of whom simultaneously belong to the ethnic majority in Finland. There the individual can choose when and where (not) to define oneself as an Adventist in the peer group. Minority membership is something that is constantly re-negotiated across a variety of situations (Rastas 2007, p. 72); this can also apply to youth of religious minorities, when the membership and minority values construct a significant dimension in life. This can generate settings with personal feelings of 'non-belonging' even when others perceive one as 'belonging'. It is contrary to, for example, the Finnish 'non-white' youth who, despite their Finnishness, in the predominantly white society may be categorized as 'strangers' with regard to 'a colouring discourse that is aimed at distinguishing those who belong from those who don't' (Rastas 2004, p. 94; see also Yuval-Davis, Anthias and Kofman [2005], p. 521]).

A relatively tight religious minority provides an interesting focus for research on minorities, both in terms of a relatively defined value system in the increasingly pluralistic society, and in terms of the role the social network of the community can play in socializing younger generations by supporting the development and maintenance of values and identity (Kuusisto 2007). Adventism, a small religious minority with some 3,800 members (under 1 per cent of the 5.2 million total population) in Finland, is here utilized as a case study context. The Lutheran tradition still remains to have a strong influence in the culture, although, like in many other Western countries, the society is increasingly secularized and religiosity privatized. Despite of the 81.7 per cent Evangelical Lutheran church membership, only 51 per cent of Finns define themselves as Lutherans, and 31 per cent as Believers (Ketola 2007). Furthermore, only a small proportion of Finns could be described as 'active believers' (Kääriäinen, Niemelä and Ketola 2005, p. 168).

Religion can play a considerable role in the process of structuring identity (Heimbrock 2001, p. 64). Tajfel (1981), p. 255) defines social identity as 'that part of an individual which derives from his [sic] knowledge of his membership of a social group (or groups) together with the value and emotional significance attached to that membership'. Consequently, *religious identity* is here understood, in line with the social identity theory, as the individual's identification as a member of a particular religious group (Greenfield and Marks 2007, p. 247); a religious social identity that consists of the perceptions and conceptions that people have concerning themselves as members of this particular religious denomination. Identification with a religion is, besides the actual religious practice, a social contact with other members of the religious community (Amyot and Sigelman 1996, p. 177). Previous research has found growing evidence of a relationship between identity commitment and an individual's sense of self-continuity (Dunkel 2005, p. 2). Van Hoof and Raaijmakers (2002) regard a sense of being the same person through time and social contexts as a central characteristic of identity formation; and, in line with the connection between identity and self-esteem utilized in Umaña-Taylor (2004), they also found a positive linear relationship between the spatial integration of identity and subjective well-being.

Identity negotiations are here understood as the moving or 'navigating' between experienced memberships and different sets of norms and *values* – as desirable, abstract goals (Knafo and Schwartz 2003, p. 595) – particularly those of the minority and the majority social settings. The unfolding nature of identity as a process of constant negotiations is especially apparent when the values and expectations in a home differ greatly from those endorsed in the wider society (Schmälzle 2001, p. 30; van Hoof and Raaijmakers 2002, p. 201), when an individual lives concurrently in different cultures (Sam and Virta 2003, p. 213), or when different traditions are present in the family (Froese 2008). Identity negotiations of minority youth have previously been studied, for instance within the Suroye young people in Sweden (Cetrez 2005).

Social capital as a social resource generated in interaction between people (e.g. Ellonen [2008], p. 31]) is here significant from the perspective of the social ties and networks created by the religious participation (Putnam 2000; Wuthnow 2002). Social networks in the Finnish Adventist community have, in my previous research (Kuusisto 2007), been found to provide support for socializing and maintaining Adventist values, norms and identity, for example in the form of intergenerational closure (Coleman 1988), thereby generating social capital for these youth and their families.

The *majority* here refers to the predominantly Lutheran Finnish mainstream population, whereas the *minority* refers to the Finns affiliated with the Adventist Church. Besides some theological dissimilarity with the Lutheranism as a majority, the main differences in the everyday life consist of the weekly Saturday Sabbath observance, including 'rest' from the everyday duties; adult baptism; and an emphasis on holistic well-being displayed in, for example, dietary choices (such as avoidance of pork and stimulants). Naturally, like any community, Adventism also contains variance between individuals, and thus positions to issues such as dietary matters differ across the denomination. In contrast to the usage of the concept 'minority' in some other contexts, it is important to note that even though Adventism as a religion is in a minority position in Finland, it does belong to Protestant Christianity like the Lutheran church. Also, in aspects other than religion, Adventists belong to the 'mainstream' in the Finnish society. They are not segregated in any particular way, do not essentially differ from the mainstream population in terms of ethnicity or appearance (e.g. particular dress), nor are they lacking any apparent power positions in the society. Thus, what is here referred to as minority membership is very much a question of the individual's personal identification, and especially for the teenagers these may be under constant re-negotiation when faced with the difference of values between the religious community and the mainstream social contexts. There are established attitude measures regarding different religious denominations in Finland, and when it comes to Adventists the results show that the general attitudes towards Adventists in Finland are fairly neutral, positioning it in the halfway point among the religious movements in the country, with 22 per cent positive, 18 per cent negative opinions (Kääriänen, Niemelä and Ketola 2005, p. 79).

My preceding quantitative analysis on the survey data of Adventist teenagers, of whom forty-six were attending a denominational and fifty-three a mainstream school, showed no statistically significant correlation between the measured religious identity and the school social context.[1] However, the answers to open-ended questions in the questionnaire (Kuusisto 2005a) provided a wider range of experiences, something that statistical data are often unable to grasp, let alone represent. These reflections brought light into some of the difficulties these youth face in negotiating the minority values and identity in a mainstream school context, which is now more closely explored with the present analysis.

Method

This article examines the social networks and identity negotiations of Finnish Adventist teenagers in diverse social contexts, as accounted for by the youth in interviews, guided by the following two-part research question:

How does religious minority versus majority position in attended school affect Finnish Adventist youth's (1) social networks; and (2) value negotiations between majority and minority identification?

The data were gathered in 2004–2005 at nationwide denominational youth summer camps, where I openly operated in a dual role of participant observer and camp counsellor.[2] The presently analysed data were gathered with semi-structured face-to-face interviews of ten Adventist teenagers (ages sixteen to seventeen), who were chosen from a wider survey data[3] on the basis of geographical distribution, equal representation of genders, and diversity in family background (e.g. both parents Adventists versus one Adventist parent), as well as attendance at mainstream versus Adventist schools. Interviews were conducted in an empty hobby room or outside; they were recorded and subsequently transcribed.[4] Conducting the interviews myself, the double role as camp staff member was likely to support trust, but – just as the researcher's position and characteristics always do – would naturally be part of how the responses were constructed in that particular situation.

The interview outline was based on the research literature, as well as my previous findings (e.g. Kuusisto [2005a; 2007]) on the same religious minority. The outline covered the following topic areas: (1) family information; (2) religious socialization in childhood (e.g. religious practices in the home); (3) current values and possible effect on life choices; (4) current relationship with congregation (e.g. participation); (5) personal religious experiences (e.g. possible conversion or baptism); (6) future plans and possible influence of religion in those.

For the analysis, the data were first reduced to the areas targeted by the research problem, then categorized thematically using the interview outline as a structural starting point. Commencing this, in the following I will first summarize the thematic analysis of the ten interviews to set the framework, then present two cases to illustrate the variation within the data and in order to shift the focus from 'an average person' to the actual people involved (Teddlie, Tashakkori and Johnson 2008, p. 403). After all, all too often the stereotypes simplify and generalize characteristics that are then used to label minority members.

Results

All ten teenagers interviewed had been brought up in relatively close affiliation to the Adventist church, although the intensity and the actual socialization practices varied in terms of family characteristics, such as whether one or two of the parents were denomination members, and due to the physical proximity and demographics (e.g. (non-)existence of similar-age peers) of the local church. Presently, most of the youth participate in church regularly, many also holding responsibilities in church services. Adventism is for all of them a significant part of life, although for some the personal devotion and its effect on life choices such as future career are more important than to others. Individual variance is notable also in terms of personal religious continuum, or the personal paths to the present situation. For instance, one of the youth had gone through a 'rough patch', using drugs and alcohol, and been away from the congregation for several years, but then had a conversion experience; whereas for most others the course of life in terms of denominational affiliation had been very steady.

Being an Adventist was generally described by these teenagers in terms of experienced affiliation rather than formal membership – perhaps since Adventist children are not christened as babies and thereby many youth from Adventist families do not (yet) hold formal membership. Adventism as such was portrayed through reference to the Sabbath, adult baptism, and health principles. Practical commitment was depicted as the involvement in congregational responsibilities (e.g. singing or accompanying in music programme, organizing children's programme; one of the teenagers had also given a sermon for the congregation).

Regarding mainstream versus denominational social contexts, here mainly brought up in terms of the social composition of attended schools, the strength of Adventist schools was seen in comfortable expression of faith and religious identity. Anna-Sofia (aged sixteen) says:

[T]here the people have the courage to speak openly about their faith and sometimes, even during the lunch hour, we just gather into the lobby and discuss religion and sometimes think about the prayer requests of the week together with some circle of friends. It's really nice then when you've got people around you that think the same way.

The experiences of being in religious minority position in a mainstream school were also generally positive, although some of the boys had been teased about their religious affiliation. Yet, in mainstream schools, the youth were repeatedly confronted with values and expectations that were in contrast to family values (see also Schmälzle [2001]; van Hoof & Raaijmakers [2002]; Sam and Virta [2003]). These involved dietary matters (e.g. when the only alternative meal included pork), different religious views (e.g. baptism, the Sabbath), the use of language (swearing), and lifestyle values (e.g. alcohol, partying). Janita (aged seventeen) says:

> J: I usually quite often disagree with others [in mainstream school] when we discuss religion.
> AK: In what kind of matters?
> J: Well. For example, you know – we've spoken about how youth behave with alcohol and all that. My school mates think that it's all completely normal. I think it is so destructive to oneself that it's absolutely no use; that it's only, you know, so harmful, so in my opinion it does not make any sense.

The differing views often caused situations in which the youth needed to make value choices. For example, when it comes to 'partying' with friends, some of the teenagers opted for staying home from such activities altogether, whereas others went along, but stayed sober; still others had sometimes used alcohol. Thus, the youth in mainstream schools faced coping with more negotiations of minority values and identity, sometimes balancing between compromising their values and being excluded or excluding themselves. Furthermore, since, of course, not all non-Adventist peers behave in a particular way, either, for example using alcohol or swearwords, those youth who 'went along sober' could sometimes find like-minded company, too.

When it comes to social networks, the data point to a principal difference between those attending a mainstream school – who thus have two parallel circles of friends, one from the school and the other from the congregation – and those attending Adventist faith schools – who describe strong ties and communality within the denominational community, but sometimes only weak links outside the denomination. This is, naturally, predictable since school takes such a large proportion of the time available, and it is only natural to associate with the schoolmate peers. Expressing and living by the shared values can intensify the experiences of social identity. All the same, having to constantly manifest and perform one's minority identity in a majority context could strengthen it in similar extent, although by different means; it may be common for members of such small minorities to have the experience of being some sort of 'living example' of the whole minority. This way, identity can also be imposed by attributions or social actions of others (Anthias 2001a, p. 837).

Of the following two cases, the first one depicts one example of childhood in a family of two Adventist parents, whereas the other pictures an experience of growing-up in a home of two different parental worldviews.

'Saana'

Saana is a sixteen-year-old girl with an older sister and two Adventist parents. They live close to one of the Adventist campuses and she goes to an Adventist school. She talks a lot about her loving and supporting family. Saana says that for her, learning about God in the home has had a big influence into her principles in life: created basic trust; produced a secure atmosphere in the home; and enabled a harmonious childhood. She adds that in their family, the very close-knit relations must be partly because God has influenced them and blessed the family.

Religion still is an important aspect in the home. The whole family gathers together in the evenings for a prayer together, as well as sharing recent events in all of their lives. They have also gone to church regularly throughout her life. On Sabbath afternoons, the family cooks lunch together and often goes outdoors for a walk or exercise. Sabbath for them is a day of togetherness.

Saana remembers only one occasion as a child when she didn't want to go to church. Her mother had replied that she did not need to go if she did not want to go. But then she says she started feeling an inner urge to go, although the mother kept saying that there's no need if she felt uneasy about going. But she says she'd have had such a bad conscience for having stayed at home. She now looks back at this as a phase when going to church was 'somewhat difficult'. Presently, however, going to church is important to her.

When the children were small, the family ate only vegetarian food; nowadays they also eat fish or chicken. Pork is not eaten, although the family agrees that it is not a question of salvation, and on rare occasions if they are visiting someone who only offers them ham pizza, in Saana's example, they might eat it. Still, she sees the chosen diet as a question of principle from which she does not like to deviate. In her opinion, God has given the dietary guidelines in the Bible for our best interest, 'not to make our life difficult ... but so that we would stay healthy.' She also realizes that many of her Adventist friends do eat 'sausage and everything in a pretty normal way', but for herself she thinks 'there have to be some principles in life. To somehow keep oneself in control.'

For Saana, being in a denominational school makes faith an important part of her life on a daily basis, as it is possible to freely discuss spiritual matters with others; she thinks her life would be very different if she had been to mainstream schools, and says she is not sure how much of her faith she would 'dare' to share in mainstream school context, whereas in the denominational school, according to her, religion is visible all the time, although she recognizes that some of the pupils there are not believers. Religion there is a topic of discussion, and 'when something happens, people consider it an answer to a prayer. [They] tell what happened and are not like, what a weird coincidence.' For her, Adventist friends are closer than others because they share a 'similar doctrinal background', and she accounts to usually always having a strong feeling of togetherness in her Adventist school or, as she says, the 'Adventist circles' in general. This is illustrated in her account on the local congregation:

> That when you enter the church and you know everyone, the older people, too, and we smile at each other and greet each other and so, also with the elderly. That it is not just your friends that you'd miss [if you went away].

Moreover, Saana also defines her minority membership through the social ties and the denominational network. She says that to her, being an Adventist means: 'That there are these people, these people in particular, around me. That ... I wouldn't be what I am if I was somewhere [else], with some other people.' She emphasizes that being a part of some other religious denomination would not make her any less of a believer, and that in other churches there are likeminded 'good believers' just like among her own denomination.

Besides the local community school-mates, Saana also knows a few other people outside the denominational networks, mainly peers that she has met in hobbies, and of whom she also accounts to having 'one friend' who is not an Adventist. Furthermore, she realizes that denominational networks are not that homogenous either, as the teenagers from Adventist homes hold different associations to the denominational values.

> But I also have one, you know, one outsider friend ... really high values although this friend is all Lutheran you know ... And then again I've got Adventist friends who're, if you can say so, off beam. So it's not up to that, necessarily, either.

To the non-Adventist peers, she has disclosed her religious affiliation and thereby familiarized herself with a couple of peers from other denominations:

> It is always really exiting, sort of, to find a friend from some other denomination, someone who is a strong believer. ... You kind of realize that they're also – you know – really believers – that they're not like [laughs] erroneous with their faith or anything. They also have some really good points.

Saana would like to get more involved with the events organized together with various Christian congregations. She doesn't really know that much of the differences between churches; for her the personal relationship with God is what matters. Saana states her priorities in life are 'of course family, friends and religion, God.' For her, Sabbath is a day of rest from the everyday worries; for resting, going to church, meeting friends (although, she laughs, she does see them every day at school, too), taking part in discussions of the church, youth Bible study classes, and spending time with her family. Saana emphasizes that she goes to church weekly, unlike 'those Lutheran youth [who] basically just go to church on Christmas.'

Saana doesn't remember ever having been teased about her religion. As an example of a difficult situation related to her conviction, she recalls a situation from her primary school years when on a team trip related to her hobby, a disco was arranged for the children as a part of the general programme. Saana remembers feeling very anxious, as she wasn't used to something like that, and she didn't really want to go there but couldn't think of an option, either. So she went with the others and sat there, feeling 'somewhat disgusted'. On the other hand, she now feels that in situations like that one may notice that people:

> talk about really every-day matters there, nothing indecent or such, that it is merely their way of spending time. That it is only that when you're not used to that so it somehow makes you anxious and you may imagine it is something very sinful although it wouldn't necessarily be so.

Regarding the then recent yellow press scoops on the suspected paedophiliac exploits alleged to have taken place some decades ago in the Adventist school she's currently attending, she describes how the mutually experienced threat from the outside further tightened the social network within the school,

> since we knew that there's nothing like that there at least now ... it just made us maybe even closer as a group just because [laughing]

everyone in the outside hated us. That it was like, we were like fighting together for [our school] or something.

The pupils of the school as well as peers in the summer camps gather there from around the country, and mutual events (e.g. choir festivals, volleyball tournaments) and international student exchange are arranged with the Adventist schools in other countries. Thereby, the close-knit denominational social network extends beyond the locality, and thereby also the generated social capital is not specific to the particular area. As an example, when Saana is talking about her plans for student years, she notes that her intended place of study is close to another Adventist church, led by a pastor that she already knows personally – she laughs warmly and says she will just call the local pastor if she gets too lonely.

'Jussi'

Jussi is a sixteen-year-old boy living in a small town where there are traditionally rather many Adventists because of a previously church-run health institution in the area. His mother is an Adventist, whereas his father is not. The mother has given Jussi and her younger sister religious home education. They haven't had a habit of holding family worships or reading religious literature at home, but the mother has taken them to the church, where they still go 'most of the times'. On the Sabbath, their mother 'does not make [us] clean up, or do other work, pick blueberries or anything like that'. As kids, their mother sometimes 'half-forced' them to church, which they disliked as it was 'a granny church' with no young people, but nowadays going to church is 'pretty voluntary' for them, and they also like going to church as their present congregation has a lot of programme for youth.

Jussi goes to a mainstream upper secondary school. In his class, there is one peer whom Jussi regards as an atheist, everyone else, except Jussi, belongs to the Lutheran Church. In the same school, however, there are some five or six other Adventists. When it comes to social networks, Jussi tells that he has two parallel circles of friends in the town in which he lives: one of school-mates and the other, a group of some ten kids, from among the denomination. Also, his school-mates know about his religious affiliation. These friends do not usually talk about it at all – Jussi says they 'couldn't care less which religion [he's] from'. However, the Saturday Sabbath has sometimes aroused questions, and he tells about answering them: 'well, I've just – I just say that it's the, you know ... the real Day of Rest, the one that is God's Day of Rest ... not the one that the Pope has changed to be on Sunday.' To which he says his friends haven't really reacted in any particular way; in Jussi's opinion they're just not interested in the topic.

However, he has sometimes been bullied about his religion; especially at the time when the previously mentioned suspected case of sexual harassment within the denomination was in the newspaper tabloids. At the time, certain peers at school called Jussi a 'paedophiliac Adventist', which he felt very offensive. Sometimes the same kids have been naming him a 'Jehovah's Witness', which irritates Jussi particularly due to the fact that the bullies are even as ignorant not to differentiate between different religious groups – this is comparable to what Modood (2005, p. 11) in the British context calls 'failure to distinguish Muslims from the rest of the 'black' population and its uncritical secular bias'.

Due to the fact that Jussi's father is not an Adventist, the family eats meat at home on a regular basis, so he does not have vegetarian lunches at school either. He also attends what he calls 'normal religious instruction', i.e. the mainstream Lutheran RE classes. He once chose to hold a presentation there on the Adventist pioneer from the denomination's early years, Ellen G. White. For that, he read some parts of White's books to gain knowledge of her writings. In the presentation he also brought up White's linkages to Adventism.

When asked how religion shows in his own life, Jussi answers:

Well, I naturally behave a bit differently from my friends. When my friends go – well, on May Day in [our town centre] there is this hill … where everybody goes for drinking, so – so – I think I was the only one there sober – no, I think there may have been a couple of others, too. … Yes, I went there to see what it's like.

Jussi does not account to feeling alone in situations like that: 'No – not really. I do manage with it', he says. He also says he sometimes uses swear words but 'rarely – when comparing to those others, for whom it is every second or third word'. He has also tasted alcohol but only under his parents' supervision.

Still, there was a period of time when Jussi had feelings of being excluded among his friends from school, namely when everyone else went to confirmation camps, had a party for relatives and received money and gifts: 'That was a bit difficult when … they all get money, you know, and everybody else had money and I didn't … that was a bit unfortunate … Well, then I did feel a bit left out.' Jussi had even considered attending the camp, although he says that he wouldn't have gone through the actual confirmation.

When asked what he thinks makes a person an Adventist, he replies that when people confess membership of a religion, they belong to it. He does not think the formal membership as such is the overriding factor: most of his friends from the denomination have not gone through baptism like Jussi has, at least not yet. Jussi himself was baptized on the same summer camp the previous year. He decided to get baptized because he felt 'this would be a good time to do it', he hadn't determined to do that when coming to the camp but the choice took final shape one evening:

> We had talked with [a pastor] ... there was a really strong feeling, in the follow-up gathering [after evening meetings], that everyone just cried and prayed, so it was there [that I made up my mind].

During the winter, he had attended a fortnightly church youth group preparing the youth to the baptismal choice. He feels that baptism made his relationship with God more intimate. Relationship with God for him conveys basic trust and the feeling of guidance in his life. He discloses that he only seldom prays:

> I never remember to. It never occurs to me to pray. Despite the times when – when I have to, then I pray. ... When one needs some special sort of guidance or help, then you feel you need to pray. When you can't make it on your own.

Jussi also feels he has received answers to his prayers. For example, when he was orienteering in a PE lesson and got lost, he prayed that God would lead him back safely – and after the prayer, he remembers getting a feeling that he should take a particular direction, which then led him straight into one of the control points.

Conclusions

The data picture the non-homogeneity and the varied routes for religious minority offspring to grow up and negotiate their belongings. In line with what Cetrez (2005) found about the Suroyo youth in Sweden, these Finnish Adventist youth also, to some extent, construct their personal ways or forms for religiosity. Although the national and religious identification (here Finnishness and Adventism) do not similarly collide as in Cetrez's sample, and the Adventist identification of these youth does not significantly vary across social contexts, the intensity of the expressions of this identification vary strongly depending on the religious composition of the social context. Furthermore, as in Cetrez's study, these youth also use strategically different patterns for negotiating their identity. Some of the interviewed Adventist youth could be described more as competent in both 'worlds', i.e. those of minority and majority, whereas others live more deeply embedded in either of the two, merely 'visiting' the other one.

As Yuval-Davis (2006) also notes, people can 'belong' in many different ways, and this identification can be an act of self-identification or identification by others. Thereby, the negotiations under scrutiny in this article describe this process of the constant re-positioning of oneself in the belongings of minority and majority, which for some of the youth form two overlapping 'circles', whereas for others these spheres are more separate. The importance of the individual's sense of self-continuity (Dunkel 2005), or spatial integration of identity – being the same person through time and social contexts (van Hoof & Raaijmakers 2002) – to personal well-being (Umaña-Taylor 2004) is illustrated with the cases presented above. Where Saana feels very anxious of breaking her personal boundaries by attending the disco, Jussi describes a very different experience of a comparable choice. This is not to say that one alternative is necessarily better than another – Saana's account is one of a happy, bright, well-being young lady, truly contented with her life – but to demonstrate how the moving between social contexts can be strenuous to youth, with values that in one way or the other differ from those of their peers.

The descriptions of the 'majority' social context bring up an interesting perspective to the variety within the society as a whole – what exactly are 'the mainstream values' to which these youth need to adapt and negotiate?[5] Besides the extensive multiplicity within what the 'majority' can stand for – including the Adventist youth themselves, in matters other than their religious affiliation – the 'religious minority' in the mainstream school peer group could also refer to those youth, regardless of the object (particular religious group) of their religious affiliation, for whom religion has personal significance in life.

The down side of attending denominational schools can be the lack of social ties outside the denomination, as these youth may thus be left lacking social capital in their neighbourhood outside of school (see also Weller [2007]). Besides, they may be lacking the practice, and thus also competencies, of dealing with the contrasting values. On the other hand, the strengthened value system, religious social identity, and strong social networks within the denomination can work as protective structures and thereby ease the transition to new settings, as long as the individual maintains the denominational ties during the first years of study or work life. In late adolescence and young adulthood, the strength of religious values and identity are likely to play an important role in future choices such as that of occupation, as well as whether or not a future spouse will be found within the same religious denomination.

The same applies to the homes with 'two cultures' in terms of differing parental worldviews; these may create both extra challenges and additional strengths in terms of value transmission, as in the two-culture families the provided options and models are likely to be less ideologically singular (see, for example, Knafo & Schwartz [2003]). If the parents disagree on some core values and thereby provide two differing models, the situation may be strenuous at times, and the children may have to navigate between their values and identities at an early age. However, perhaps these youth also hold more 'accepted' choices or more concrete options for value systems when there is diversity already within the family. Such dual membership could also foster stronger cultural competencies (Rastas 2007, p. 16) and the ability to synthesize the multiple belongings, and thereby create a new, personal way of being a young Adventist in Finland (related to discussion on hybrid or hyphenated identities), rather than falling between the two cultures (Anthias 2001b).

Whether the individual's position is distinctive by religion, ethnicity or something else, it is valuable to grow up understanding two (or more) cultures, having heterogeneous social contacts and networks, and gaining experiences of various social contexts. This can facilitate the development of competencies and acquisition of knowledge on other worldviews, religions, and cultures, all of which are needed for intercultural and interfaith dialogue, as well as for constructing one's personal value system and identity. Finally, diverse social encounters can build towards equality by making the individual realize how the 'outsider friend [also has] really high values' (*Saana*; as quoted above); and thereby prevent too limited views on 'the other' – on both sides.

Notes

1. Survey utilized research design parallel to Umaña-Taylor (2004), including *Multi-group Ethnic Identity Measure* MEIM (Phinney 1992; 2004) amended to the Finnish Adventist context. School type correlation with identity (MEIM) was .16 (for direct identity statement .10). (Kuusisto 2005a).

2. See Kuusisto 2005b for more on data gathering and sample.

3. The Finnish Adventist Church membership register at the time held 304 youth between fourteen and eighteen years of age. Out of the total respondents (n =125), the analyses included those who reported having at least one Adventist parent (n =100; 56 (per cent) females and 44 (per cent) males). Of these, seventy-nine teenagers have two Adventist parents, twenty-one have one Adventist and other (a) Lutheran (three mothers, six fathers), (b) not member of any church (three mothers, seven fathers), or (c) parental church membership (two fathers) is unknown. Participants were between the ages thirteen and nineteen (f =3, 17, 28, 21, 16, 11, 4 for 13–19, respectively), the average being 15.8.

4. Interviews were conducted in Finnish; quotations translated by the researcher.

5. Floya Anthias referred to similar question in her keynote lecture in *Generations in flux – international interdisciplinary conference on ethnicity, integration and family ties* (Helsinki, 23–24 October 2008) by problematizing the existence of some sort of 'core' of dominant society to which the immigrants are supposed to be assimilated, noting that the society itself is exceedingly heterogeneous.

References

AMYOT, ROBERT P. and SIGELMAN, LEE 1996 'Jews without Judaism? Assimilation and Jewish identity in the United States', *Social Science Quarterly*, vol. 77, no. 1, pp. 177–89
ANTHIAS, FLOYA 2001a 'The concept of "social division" and theorising social stratification: looking at ethnicity and class', *Sociology*, vol. 35, no. 4, pp. 835–54
—— 2001b 'New hybridities, old concepts: the limits of "culture"', *Ethnic and Racial Studies*, vol. 24, no. 4, pp. 619–41
CETREZ, ÖNVER 2005 *Meaning-Making Variations n Acculturation & Ritualization: A Multi-Generational Study of Suroyo Migrants in Sweden*, Uppsala: Uppsala Universitet
COLEMAN, JAMES S. 1988 'Social capital in the creation of human capital', *The American Journal of Sociology*, vol. 94, Supplement: Organizations and Institutions: Sociological and Economic Approaches to the Analysis of Social Structure (1988), pp. S95–S120
DUNKEL, CURTIS S. 2005 'The relation between self-continuity and measures of identity', *Identity: An International Journal of Theory and Research*, vol. 5, no. 1, pp. 21–34
ELLONEN, NOORA 2008 *Kasvuyhteisö nuorten turvana. Sosiaalisen pääoman yhteys nuorten masentuneisuuteen ja rikekäyttäytymiseen [Local Community as a Source of Security for Youth: Association between Social Capital, Depression and Delinquency]*, Tampere: Tampere University Press
FRANKENBERG, RUTH 1993 *White Women, Race Matters: The Social Construction of Whiteness*, Minneapolis, MN: University of Minnesota Press
FROESE, REGINE 2008 'One family, two religions: child belief or child grief in Christian-Muslim families?', *British Journal of Religious Education*, vol. 30, no. 1, pp. 37–47
GREENFIELD, EMILY A. and MARKS, NADINE F. 2007 'Religious social identity as an explanatory factor for associations between more frequent formal religious participation and psychological well-being', *International Journal for the Psychology of Religion*, vol. 17, no. 3, pp. 245–59
HEIMBROCK, HANS-GÜNTER 2001 '"Religious identity" between home and transgression', *Journal of Education and Religion*, vol. 2, no. 1, pp. 63–78
HELVE, HELENA 2002 *Arvot, muutos ja nuoret [Values, change and youth]*, Helsinki: Yliopistopaino
JAY, GREGORY 2007 'Who invented white people?', in Robert P. Yagelski (ed.), *The Thomson Reader: Conversations in Context*, Boston, MA: Thomson/Heinle, pp. 96–102
JOSEPH, CYNTHIA 2006 'Negotiating discourses of gender, ethnicity and schooling: ways of being Malay, Chinese and Indian schoolgirls in Malaysia', *Pedagogy, Culture & Society*, vol. 14, no. 1, pp. 35–53
KÄÄRIÄINEN, KIMMO, NIEMELÄ, KATI and KETOLA, KIMMO 2005 *Religion in Finland: Decline, Change and Transformation of Finnish Religiosity*, Tampere: Publications of the Church Research Institute
KETOLA, KIMMO 2007 'Suomalaisten uskonnollinen identiteetti' ['Religious identity of the Finns'], *Kirkkomonitor 2007*, http://www.uskonnot.fi/raportit/?year=2007
KNAFO, ARIEL and SCHWARTZ, SHALOM H. 2003 'Parenting and adolescents' accuracy in perceiving parental values', *Child Development*, vol. 74, no. 2, pp. 595–611
KROGER, JANE 2004 *Identity in Adolescence: The Balance between Self and Other*, London: Routledge
KUUSISTO, ARNIIKA 2005a 'How does school social context affect religious minority identity: exploratory study on Adventist young people in Finland', in Siegfried Kiefer and Thomas Peterseil (eds), *Analysis of Educational Policies in a Comparative Perspective*, Linz: Universitätsverlag Rudolf Trauner, pp. 73–87

———— 2005B 'Methodological issues and challenges in studying young people's religious identity', in Helena Helve (ed.), *Mixed Methods in Youth Research*, Helsinki: Finnish Youth Research Network/Society, pp. 197–212

———— 2007 'religious identity based social networks as facilitators of teenagers' social capital: a case study on Adventist families in Finland', in Helve Helena and Bynner John (eds), *Youth and Social Capital*, London: Tufnell Press, pp. 87–102

MODOOD, TARIQ 2005 'Muslims, religious equality and secularism', Paper presented at Migration, Religion and Secularism – A Comparative Approach, Sorbonne University, Paris, 17–18 June

PHINNEY, JEAN S. 1992 'The multi-group ethnic identity measure: a new scale for use with adolescents and young adults from diverse groups', *Journal of Adolescent Research*, no. 7, 156–76

———— 2004 'The Multi-group Ethnic Identity Measure (MEIM) (Updated), http://www.calstatela.edu/academic/psych/html/phinney.htm [version of 15.6.2004 utilized in the study]

PUTNAM, ROBERT D. 2000 *Bowling Alone: The Collapse and Revival of American Community*, New York: Simon & Schuster

RASTAS, ANNA 2004 'Am I still "white"? Dealing with the colour trouble', *Balayi: Culture, Law and Colonialism*, vol. 6, pp. 94–106

———— 2007 *Rasismi lasten ja nuorten arjessa. Transnationaalit juuret ja monikulttuuristuva Suomi [Racism in the Everyday of Children and Youth. Transnational Roots and the Increasingly Multicultural Finland]*, Nuorisotutkimusverkosto/seura, julkaisuja 78, Tampere: Tampere University Press

SAM, DAVID LACKLAND and VIRTA, ERKKI 2003 'Intergenerational value discrepancies in immigrant and host-national families and their impact on psychological adaptation', *Journal of Adolescence*, no. 26, 213–31

SCHMÄLZLE, UDO F. 2001 'The importance of schools and families for the identity formation of children and adolescents', *International Journal of Education and Religion*, 106, vol. II–1, pp. 27–42

TAJFEL, HENRI 1981 *Human Groups and Social Categories*, Cambridge: Cambridge University Press

TEDDLIE, CHARLES, TASHAKKORI, ABBAS and JOHNSON, BURKE 2008 'Emergent techniques in the gathering and analysis of mixed methods data', in Sharlene Nagy Hesse-Biber and Patricia Leavy (eds), *Handbook of Emergent Methods*, New York: Guilford Press, pp. 389-413

UMAÑA-TAYLOR, ADRIANA 2004 'Ethnic identity and self-esteem: examining the role of social context', *Journal of Adolescence*, vol. 27, pp. 139–46

VAN HOOF, ANNE and RAAIJMAKERS, QUINTEN A. W. 2002 'The spatial integration of adolescent identity: its relation to age, education, and subjective well-being', *Scandinavian Journal of Psychology*, vol. 43, pp. 201–12

WELLER, SUSIE 2007 'Managing the move to secondary school: the significance of children's social capital', in Helena Helve and John Bynner (eds), *Youth and Social Capital*, London: Tufnell Press, pp. 107–25

WUTHNOW, ROBERT 2002 'Religious involvement and status-bridging social capital', *Journal for the Scientific Study of Religion*, vol. 41, December 2002, pp. 669–84

YUVAL-DAVIS, NIRA 2006 'Belonging and the politics of belonging', *Patterns of Prejudice*, vol. 40, no. 3, pp. 197–214

YUVAL-DAVIS, NIRA, ANTHIAS, FLOYA and KOFMAN, ELEONORE 2005 'Secure borders and safe haven and the gendered politics of belonging: beyond social cohesion', *Ethnic and Racial Studies*, vol. 28, no. 3, pp. 513–35

Transnational family relationships, social networks and return migration among British-Caribbean young people

Tracey Reynolds

Abstract

The study explores the issue of transnational family relationships and return migration among British-Caribbean second generation young people.[1] It describes how transnational family ties and social networks are utilized as social capital resources to facilitate these young people's migration from Britain to the Caribbean, their parents' country of origin. A combination of internally formed and externally imposed understandings of ethnic identity, home and belonging are also important factors influencing these young people's decision to migrate to the Caribbean, alongside other pragmatic and practical reasons. Drawing on in-depth interviews with a qualitative sample of second generation return migrants residing in Jamaica, the discussion reflects on how these young people manage their adjustment and settlement. It also explores the gendered nature of their experiences of return migration.

Introduction

The study explores the issue of transnational family relationships and return migration among British-Caribbean second generation young people. It describes how transnational family ties and social networks are utilized as social capital resources to facilitate these young people's migration from Britain to the Caribbean, their parents' country of origin. A combination of internally formed and externally imposed understandings of ethnic identity, home and belonging are also important factors influencing these young people's decision to migrate to the Caribbean, alongside other pragmatic and practical reasons. Drawing on in-depth interviews with a qualitative sample of second generation return migrants residing in Jamaica, the discussion reflects on how these young people manage their adjustment and settlement. It also explores the gendered nature of their experiences of return migration.

The Caribbean population in Britain has a well established history, emerging out of a period of mass migration from the Commonwealth Caribbean territories to the UK between the late 1940s and early 1960s (Owen 2006). The long period of settlement by this migrant group raises important questions about the ways in which the second (and subsequent) generation experience their transnational ties and family connections to the Caribbean. For instance, what are these young people's understandings of their parents' homeland? How do they construct and position their ethnic identity in relation to these cultural and familial bonds? How strong and extensive are these young people's ties to their parents' country of origin? And finally, does the second generation have any expectation or intention of return migration to the Caribbean? Whilst it is certainly true that attachment to their parents' homeland is weakening with the second generation, research suggests that some young people are, to varying degrees, maintaining strong cultural and familial ties to Caribbean (Sutton 2004; Goulbourne et al. 2010). Specifically, in the British-Caribbean context, this has led to the eventual return 'home' among a small number of young people.

The first part of the discussion highlights the views of second generation young people in Britain with strong family ties to the Caribbean. The main focus of debate is the small but distinct group of young people that decided to leave England and migrate to the Caribbean. To this end, the analysis considers the young people's motivation for return migration, including the social context in Britain. In particular, Robert Putnam's (2000; 2007) ideas concerning bonding social capital provide the basis for investigating how Caribbean young people utilize their family and social networks to make connections across geographical distance, and the extent to which these networks constitute a resource and form a kind of capital that enable individuals to eventually return.

Research background

To date, much of the empirical studies on second generation return migration across diverse ethnic and migrant groups is concerned with investigating the significance of disapora and transnationalism in the return migration process (Levitt 2001; Baldassar 2001; Foner 2002; Levitt and Waters 2002; Glick-Schiller 2004; Christou 2006, Wessendorf 2007; King and Christou 2008). In the Caribbean context, research has tended to emphasize first generation return migration – see, for example, Gmelch (1980, 1992), Thomas-Hope (1992), Bryon (2000), Abenaty (2001), Goulbourne (2002) and Chamberlain (2006). Increasingly, however, research on second generation return migration is coming to the fore. For example, a number of studies drawing from Britain, Canada and the US explore the social and cultural adjustments experienced by second generation return migrants (Bryon 1999; Plaza 2000; Duval 2002; Phillips and Potter 2005; Potter, Conway and Phillips 2005; Bauer and Thompson 2006; Potter and Phillips 2006a, 2006b; Fog-Olwig 2007). This descriptive study seeks to build on and complement the growing body of work on in this field.

In total forty-eight qualitative interviews took place with Caribbean young people of British nationality and citizenship. This was over a four-year period from 2003 to 2007.[2] The sample was drawn from several UK cities (Birmingham, Manchester, London and Notting-ham) and the Caribbean countries of Barbados, Guyana, Jamaican and St. Kitts and Nevis. In the latter context, formal discussions were also held with officials in the Facilitation Unit for Returning Nationals in Barbados and the Jamaican Returning Residents Facilitation Unit. Discussions also took place with civil servants in related government departments in Guyana and St. Kitts and Nevis. The sample criteria were that the research participants had family members living in the Caribbean and they had visited the Caribbean within the past five years. Given the specific nature of the research criteria, access to the research sample was achieved through a 'snowballing' method (Gilbert 1994). The participants ranged from sixteen to thirty years old, and involved a sample of twenty-six women and twenty-two men. Thirty of the participants had a university degree or vocational/technical qualifications. Twenty-two participants were parents with primary or school-age children (including ten lone-mothers). Although the analysis is based on the views and experiences of all of those interviewed in the respective research sites of Britain and the Caribbean, for illustrative purposes I highlight the interviews which took place with eighteen Caribbean second generation return migrants in Jamaica, specifically the three neighbouring northern-eastern coastal parishes of Saint Ann, Saint Mary and Portland,[3] areas which have a high concentration of tourism.

Across the respective Caribbean research sites, it was difficult to collect official quantifiable data that demonstrated the scale and breadth of second generation return migration from Britain. Policy officials were largely concerned with the monitoring of first generation return migrants from Britain and an assessment of the social impact of this (Planning Institute 2004). During the research fieldwork in Jamaica, for example, the Returning Resident Facilitation Unit could not provide sufficient statistical data on the proportion of second generation return residents, although similar information about the first generation return migrants was readily available. The difficulties encountered in collecting quantitative data resonated with other research projects exploring this issue of British-Caribbean second generation return migration (Potter, Conway and Phillips 2005).

Transnational identity, 'home' and belonging

A number of studies identify that transnational connections to the homeland among the first generation remain strong over time across diverse migrant communities, but these ties are weakened with the next and successive generations (Levitt 2001; Sutton 2004; Kasinitz et al. 2008). Yet, the work of Grillo (2008) suggests the growing significance of globalization and transnationalism mean that this generational distinction is too simplistic and matters are now more complex. In contemporary Europe, for instance, migrants, many of their offspring and subsequent generations are embedded into a set of personal and social relationships which connect place of birth, ancestral homeland and diaspora (Foner 2002; Glick-Schiller 2004; Christou 2006; King and Christou 2008). Wessendorf's (2007, p. 1084) study of return migration among second generation Italians in Switzerland also suggests that these social and personal relationships create a 'third space', which enable second generation young migrants to articulate an understanding of identity, home and belonging.

In my own study, many of the British-Caribbean young people questioned on their meaning of identity, home and belonging tended to forge a collective identity based on notions of the Caribbean diaspora. When defining their ethnic identity, some of the participants emphasized their familial and cultural connection to the Caribbean region as a whole or to a specific country in the region. Their understandings of ethnic identity was also influenced by the combined factors of local residence, transnational kinship ties, and the experience (or perception) of racism and social disadvantage in Britain. One participant, Makesha, made this point very clearly in her reply to a question about identity:

> I know that I'm British because that's what it says on my passport but I don't feel accepted in England because I'm black and I know that black people are treated differently here. We're made to feel that we're tolerated but not completely accepted and we're not treated equally. I know that I'm not really Jamaican in the sense that I wasn't born out there but I still choose to identify culturally with them because my parents are Jamaican and everything is done in a Jamaican style at home and so it's what I feel more comfortable

associating myself with them. (Makesha, interview location: London, October 2003)

When similarly questioned about issues of identity, home and belonging, Keisha also highlights the importance of her cultural ties and transnational family relationships:

I would say my family is important to me. They give me my cultural identity, my Caribbean identity.
Q: How do you define a Caribbean identity?
That's tricky one, I just am. It's who I am and my way of being and I think it's my family that give my 'Caribbean-ness'. I'm not sure that word exists but you get what I'm trying to say, don't you? My family make me the person I am today and my identity comes through that family history and cultural heritage. We live in different parts of the world, Jamaica, Canada and England, but to me that's not important because we all identify with each other because of our history. We have a natural affinity, a connection that doesn't have to be explained. Just knowing that they're out there supporting me helps me to understand who I am. (Keisha, interview location: Birmingham, February 2004)

Social capital, as a theoretical concept, helps us to analyse how families represent an important resource in generating networks and relationships of trust and reciprocity across transnational fields.[4] Robert Putnam (2000), a leading figure in social capital debates, suggests that social networks found in families are valued for binding communities and societies together. These social networks provide the basis for social cohesion, solidarity and civic participation. Other writers in the field also suggest issues of reciprocal trust, social support and social connectedness, typically understood as key features of social capital; also represent important social resources within family relationships (Morrow 2001; Winter 2002; Edwards, Franklin and Holland 2003). Ties of trust and reciprocity emerging through family relationships enable social capital to be built up over time and transmitted across generations (Zontini 2004; Franklin 2007). Family bonds are themselves utilized as a social resource by individuals in the construction of their ethnic identity (Reynolds 2006a; 2006b; Goulbourne et al. forthcoming).

Strong bonding ties of ethnic and cultural identity emerged in many participants' accounts. Those young people who expressed extensive and strong ties to the Caribbean were more likely to participate in transnational family activities, such as family visits 'home' and the family reunion in the Caribbean (Reynolds 2006a). The frequency of family visits and holidays to the Caribbean was encouraged by the relatively affordability of air travel. A few participants also remembered frequent childhood visits made to their grandparents in the Caribbean during the British school summer holidays. This arrangement provided Daniel with cherished memories with his grandparents and cousins in Jamaica:

> Every summer she [mum] sent me to stay with grandparents and cousins in JA until I was about fifteen. Every summer my grandmother looked after me. My cousins and would pick oranges and ackee off the tree with my grandmother, and we'd help her prepare food. Every Saturday morning, I'd have to get up early and go to the market, with my gran, shopping. (Daniel, interview location: Manchester, November 2003)

Such family visits were regarded by these young people as an important resource in maintaining their family ties to the Caribbean, and strengthened their transnational relationships and cultural ties to the region. In recent years, new and advanced forms of telecommunication systems, such as emails, internet and webcams, also resulted in increased frequency of contact with family members residing there.

It is important to bear in mind that important interplay exists between internally formed and externally imposed constructions of home and belonging among the participants. The former, as I suggest above, emerges through the second generation's cultural attachment to the Caribbean and their participation in transnational family networks. The latter, however, emerges through Caribbean young people's perception of a racially subordinate status in Britain. There is little doubt that despite suffering ethnic penalties in education and the labour market, second generation Caribbeans in Britain have experienced economic success and social mobility compared to their first generation parents (Platt 2005; Cheung and Heath 2007; Heath 2008). Research emerging from the US similarly finds that second generation Caribbeans are doing much better than their parents on many measures (Waters 1999; Farley and Alba 2002; Kasinitz et al. 2008). However, many of the participants interviewed for this study believed that second generation Caribbeans in Britain had not generally progressed as well their North American counterparts.

Commonly remarked upon by the participants was the feeling that they faced limited social and economic opportunities as part of their everyday lives in Britain. This placed restrictions on their ambitious and expectations for social and economic success, and motivated return migration among some of the young people. For example, Nathaniel and Roystone described the frustrations they experienced in Britain and the way in which they viewed return migration as a viable and strategic route towards economic and social success:

It's hard to get ahead in business and life as a black man, not impossible but much harder. As a black man, qualifications will only get you so far, but if you're a militant black man like me then you're always going to meet stumbling blocks. Many white people will always try to stop you from getting ahead because they don't like to see a black man climbing the business ladder too far and too quickly. In England too many people feel very threatened by successful black men. That's why I decided to leave. I got sick and tired of the system and trying to play white man's game way by the white man's rules. Every day was a struggle for me to get ahead and make something of my life. There are more opportunities in Jamaica to do so and my only regret is that I had not come here sooner right after I graduated university. (Nathaniel, interview location: Jamaica, July 2007)

Loads of my white friends in London, I tried to talk to them but they didn't really don't understand the realities of being a black man. I never felt comfortable in my own skin in England. But in Jamaica I'm comfortable in my own skin. I'm a very hard worker. I can hustle for a living and if you come to Jamaica with that attitude to work hard, then there are more options here for you to build your own business. I'm in a better position now to invest in a good future for my family. I wasn't in a position to that in London. (Roystone, interview location: Jamaica, May 2004)

Improved quality of life was another issue that motivated return migration among the young people, and several parents felt that return migration would benefit their children. This was the case of Beverley, a single-mother, living in Jamaica for two years. Beverley took the return migration by her first generation parents as an opportunity to herself return. Beverley's concern for son's well-being and his poor schooling performance in England were crucial factors in her decision to migrate to Jamaica, as she comments below:

When we lived in Handsworth [Birmingham], my son, Jerome, got in with the wrong crowd at schools and I could see that a negative path in life was being set out for him. He was expelled from one school and then another. The schools in the area had already labelled him as a trouble-maker because of the crowd he was moving with. When mum and dad announced they were finally going home, I thought 'right that's it, my prayers have been answered, here's my chance to follow them out there to make a better life for Jerome'. I didn't know much about Jamaica other than going there on holidays but I knew the schools were decent and that the teachers were very strict and he needed that discipline. He's really excelled now and come into his own with his schooling. (Beverley, interview location: Jamaica, August 2007)

Tanya, also reflects that a deciding factor in her return was to seek an improved quality of life for her children:

> Culturally I wanted them to experience the Caribbean values I grew up with, and grow up with a strong identity. Where better for them to learn than by living in Jamaica and the Caribbean as a whole? We live in a small community, and people still make time to talk to you and keep an eye out for the children. They have much more space to breathe; they're outside more getting plenty of fresh air and exercise. And Sundays is beach day, which the children love. (Tanya, interview location: Jamaica, June 2004)

It is perhaps an interesting paradox that first generation migrants came to Britain in search of better opportunities for social and economic success, and also the desire for an improved quality of life. Yet, the second generation migrants interviewed are motivated to return to the Caribbean to achieve these same ambitions. This raises the question as to whether second generation return migration represents the comparative failure of inter-generational social mobility among Caribbean migrants in Britain. Or does return migration represent the particular strengths of Caribbean transnational family relationships and its success in encouraging a form of reverse migration across the generations? Perhaps, a third dimension to consider is that the vast majority of second generation Caribbeans in Britain do not demonstrate any expectation or intention of return migration, and some who intend to do so never get around to doing this. As I highlighted earlier, it is only a small number of Caribbean young people that have considered return migration, and fewer still that have the opportunity and resources to do so. The next section of the analysis looks at some of the related factors that enable a small minority of Caribbean young people to translate an expectation of return migration into reality. The discussion particularly highlights the role of family networks as an important social capital resource in motivating and facilitating return migration.

Family networks, social capital and return migration

The young people's participation in Caribbean transnational family networks, alongside their perception of social disadvantage experienced in Britain, represented recurrent themes in the analysis. As previously highlighted, all of the participants had very strong family ties to the Caribbean region and made frequent visits to the region.

These second generation return migrants had, prior to return, visited their Caribbean country of destination on at least three occasions over a five-year period. Most of these participants had first generation parents who had similarly returned home after reaching retirement age in England. Other factors also characterized these second generation return migrants. For instance, they tended to be lone- or married parents with pre-school children. In addition, three-quarters of the sample of second generation return migrants held university degrees from British higher education institutions (or professional–vocational qualifications) and a further 90 per cent were working in full-time paid employment prior to migration.

The commonality of characteristics among these second generation return migrants confirms Potter's claim (2005, p. 14) that 'return migrants are best viewed as people endowed with social capital, potential and realized'. Importantly, the second generation migrants each had existing family networks and social resources that they drew on to facilitate their return migration. Many of the participants recognized that their first generation parents' return migration to the country of origin provided them with the opportunity, networks and resources to similarly migrate:

> Mum and dad were living out there for around twelve years before we moved out there, so that made the transition a bit easier for us and because we had visited a few times before we moved out, we sort of knew that it wouldn't be easy for us because we'd have to adapt to a completely different lifestyle. Luckily mum and dad set us up with everything to get us started. We lived with them for the first year until we found our feet. It really helped ease us into our new lives. A big plus for us was that my parents are quite well known in the village. When we lived with them we were always meeting new people, and building up new contacts. It was a Godsend because we wouldn't know where to start if they had been there to open doors for us. (Monica, interview location: Jamaica, August 2007)

Not all of the second generation return migrants regarded their migration as a long-term permanent move. Some of the participants saw their return migration in temporary terms. In the following example, Sandra, a single-mother, who had migrated to Jamaica three years previously, reflects that practical and pragmatic reasons were behind her decision to migrate to the Caribbean on a temporary basis. This was the need for family members to provide cheap childcare during her children's formative years. Sandra planned to eventually re-migrate to England when her children reached secondary school age and she did not require similar levels of childcare:

In England I struggled with childcare costs because I didn't get any financial help from their father. Mummy was asking me to come live out here, [Jamaica]. I wasn't so sure at first because I was terrified of the serious upheaval to my life. I asked myself "How would I fit in coming from a completely different society?" and "How would my children adjust?" But financially it was a no-brainer. It made sense because there's a network of aunties and cousins who I can call on to help and there's mummy who's always available to care for the children. It took me six months to pack up my life in England. I haven't regretted the move yet because the cost of living is so much cheaper. I will go back [to England] when the children get older and they can look after themselves more, but for now Saint Mary [Jamaican parish] is home. (Sandra, interview location: Jamaica, August 2007)

The second generation return migrants utilized social capital notions of trust, social support and connectedness, found within their kinship ties, to assist them with settlement an adjustment in the country of destination. For example, they utilized the contacts and knowledge of family members to help them plan the more practical aspects of their return. This included building or purchasing a new home, finding paid employment or seeking out other business opportunities, and assistance with duty and tax concessions. The social contacts that emerged through their family ties were particularly instrumental in helping them to find paid employment. Typically in the Caribbean, a cultural practice exists whereby paid work is secured through people's informal social networks and a reliance upon reciprocal trust relationships built up over time. The example of Sherry, who migrated to Jamaica nine months ago, was one of several examples who found employment on the basis of their kin members' reciprocal trust relationships within the local community:

I was clueless about finding work and how the system works. My aunt invited me over to her house, her friend was there and auntie said "Do you know anyone looking to hire my niece?" Her friend said "Yes definitely, because you're Miss Walker's family and so I will help you." Then later that evening she phoned me and said "I need some help at the clinic, so come in tomorrow." I asked if I come with a copy of my CV [curriculum vitae] and she was like 'No, no, it's problem, you're Miss Walker's niece. She's a good woman and I trust her completely. She recommended you and that's all I need to know." Anyway, that's how I got my first job as a health adviser. (Sherry, interview location: Jamaica, August 2007)

Mark, interviewed in 2003, also explains how he utilized the contacts of native-born family to ensure he was not financially exploited when it was time to build his new home:

Uncle Winston said to me, "When you go to negotiate the price for the cement blocks with the contractors, whatever you do, make sure one of your cousins go with you, so that they can see you're someone who got family in the community. Otherwise the contractors, they will see you're from 'foreign'[5] and will try to extort money from you." If people know you're related to someone in the community they won't con you. (Mark, interview location: Jamaica, July 2003)

Although there were many examples of care, support and reciprocal trust – all vital components of social capital – coming from the family network, there were other examples whereby family members exploited these social capital expectations of care, support and reciprocal trust to take advantage of the second generation return migrants:

My cousin lost her job and because she had some financial problems I loaned her the money. But she was always borrowing money from me and I had to stop loaning her. Then we were faced with the problem of all the lies and malicious rumours she started spreading about me and husband. She was saying "they come from 'foreign' with all their money and think they're better than we [native born kin]". It caused bad feeling in the family and I decided we needed to distance ourselves from them. Families can be strength but they can also be a burden. (Georgia, interview location: Jamaica, July 2004)

As the examples of Mark and Georgia suggest, the second generation return migrants were sometimes marked out as 'foreign' or 'outsiders' by the native-born kin and community members. The next section of the analysis considers the implications of the second generation return migrants 'outsider' status in terms of cultural adjustment and settlement. It specifically considers the gendered nature of their experiences of return migration.

Adjustment and relationships

The English accent and being British-born firmly established the young return migrants as 'outsiders' within their local community. This created advantages and disadvantages for them in terms of their experiences of return migration. Regarding the advantages, many of the second generation return migrants were able to utilize their English accent as a social capital resource in generating wider economic and employment opportunities. Several of the young people expressed that it was relatively easy for them to secure business loans to start up businesses in regions dominated by overseas tourism. They believed that not only did the English accent still characterize notions of an upper-middle class status in Jamaica but also, among financiers, there was a common perception that an English accent would attract a steady supply of English, North American and other European tourists. At the time of the research fieldwork, six of the participants were working for large corporate hotels in receptionist/front-of-house posts. Interestingly, all of them acknowledged that their English accent was instrumental in them securing these posts because of the perception among native-born and overseas business people that an English accent established a professional atmosphere and would attract greater numbers of affluent and foreign customers to the place of business. These findings support research undertaken by Potter and Phillips (2006a, p. 78) on second generation return migration to Barbados. This work highlighted the 'power of the English accent', its symbolic association to whiteness in Caribbean postcolonial discourses and the resulting social and economic privilege that emerged from second generation return migrants having an English accent.

Yet, despite of some of the advantages gained in the business and employment field, it would be misleading to suggest return migration was positively experienced by all. Many of the participants recognized that they would be viewed as 'outsiders' by the native-born residents and some of their family members. In addition, they were not fully prepared for the difficulties they would encounter in terms of cultural adjustment. This was particularly an issue for the young women who expressed concerns about how to conform to gender-related cultural expectations and practices in their everyday daily lives. A number of the female participants remarked that, outside of family contexts, employment and church-related activities, it was very difficult to socialize with other women in public spaces.[6] Rum shops and bars were exclusively male-defined and masculine spaces, while restaurants were viewed as family-centred arenas. These women's social lives were much home-centred compared to their lives in Britain, and they experienced greater feelings of isolation and alienation.[7] Monica, who is married with two children and has been living in Jamaica for seven years, was one of several of the female participants who reflected on the personal costs of migration and the way in which she sacrificed her own personal happiness to benefit her children. She comments:

You make your life for your kids, so whatever sadness I feel, because I do get lonely sometimes, I dry my tears because I can see how much the move has been good for the children. They love it here and have settled in really well. There are opportunities here for them to enjoy the simple things in life; they walk to school on their own. They're always playing out on the lane. I would never allow them to do that in London. And I have peace of mind because I'm not constantly worrying about their safety. (Monica, interview location Jamaica: July 2004)

Many of the second generation female return migrants identified that cultural differences and their 'outsider' status also made it difficult to establish close friendship bonds with the native-born women. Commenting on these cultural differences, Beverley claims:

I have loads of acquaintances, I know lots of people that I've met in church, and stuff like that. But friends? I don't have many. I'm different. We just think too differently, and because of that I have a problem communicating with them on a genuine level. (Beverley, interview location: Jamaica, August 2007)

Similarly, Denise, an unmarried return migrant, also highlighted that the return migrants' 'outsider' status combined with the 'power of the English accent' (Potter and Philips 2006a, p. 78) resulted in sexual competition between the two groups of women. This issue made it harder for her to establish friendships with the native-born women:

Being English you're definitely more at an advantage though because you don't have to be the prettiest or [wearing] expensive designer clothes because your accent alone can carry you through. The men love the accent and that you stand out and are different. The women can't stand it because they may be really pretty but they can never get the accent and they hate it! (Denise, interview location: Jamaica, August 2004)

Many of these women developed survival strategies to compensate for their 'outsider' status and feelings of isolation and loneliness. Socializing and networking with other second generation return migrants was one resource described by the women. Another important resource was the social support provided by family and friends back in Britain. In the example below, Patricia, who migrated to Jamaica as a teenager and has lived there for ten years, describes her reliance on frequent contact with her siblings in Britain as her social support network:

My sister lives in Tottenham [London] and we're in contact every day. If we're not on the phone then we're on the Internet, messaging each other. Fortunately my business means I'm coming back to England every six months, so I still keep up with all my friends there and I don't feel like I'm missing out and it's so easy to send a quick email or IM [instant messenge] just to say "Hi what's up?" I'm always persuading my sister, brother and my best friends to come out and visit me and they do so. Someone is here every summer. I have quite a network of people in England to call on when I need it. (Patricia, interview location: Jamaica, June 2003)

Frustrations around the lack of friendship and social bonds outside of family networks were not issues commonly experienced by the male second generation return migrants. Part of this could be attributed to the different ways in which male and female friendship bonds are formed. Female friendships stress the significance of emotional and intimacy bonds, and the value in 'being there' for each other. Male friendships, in contrast, are more social, recreational and instrumental, lacking the focus on intimacy connections (Adams and Allan 1998; Pahl and Pevalin 2005; Reynolds 2007). The majority of the male participants identified that they were able to quickly establish friendship networks with native-born men within their local communities. These men's ability to negotiate public spaces and participate in many aspects of social life assisted this process. The rum shops, bars, beachfront life, the cultural practice of 'liming' (hanging out on the street) and their participation in sporting clubs, such as the local football and cricket teams, encouraged contact with the native-born men in ways that were not so readily accessible to the female participants. Importantly, these men's status as a 'outsiders' did not pose any real difficulties for them in terms of cultural adjustment and establishing local bonds and networks within the community.

Conclusion

The study explores the extent to which Caribbean second generation young people in Britain participate and are embedded into transnational family networks. For some Caribbean young people, family and kinship relationships represent an important social capital resource in maintaining emotional, cultural and spiritual ties to the Caribbean. A small number of Caribbean young people who demonstrate strong and extensive transnational family ties have found ways to utilize these networks to assist them with return migration to their parents' country of origin. Of course, it is important to acknowledge that many Caribbean second generation young people in Britain do not demonstrate strong and extensive transnational family ties compared to their first generation parents. Moreover, many of them have lives and kinship relationships that are firmly established in Britain, and as such they do not express this expectation of return migration. Whilst this study may not represent the majority view of second generation Caribbeans in Britain, it is nonetheless important to understand the views, experiences and motivations guiding the 'silent minority' of young people that have decided to return to their parents' homeland.

Contextualized meanings around notions of identity, home and cultural belonging are central to understanding these young people's experiences. The research data suggests that much of their understanding of 'home' involves interplay between internally formed and externally imposed formed understandings. The former relates to self-definitions framed around cultural and familial attachment to the region; whilst the latter reflects their feelings of a racially subordinate status in Britain, and the discrimination they continue to encounter, despite social advances made by the second generation over the first generation. As the data highlights, return migration is motivated by the desire for an improved quality of life and economic success among many of the research participants. The data also illustrates that social capital resources generated through the family are instrumental in facilitating the participants' return migration. The participants were able to call upon the additional resources of their English accent and employment skills and qualifications gained in England to establish further social and employment opportunities in their country of destination. However, their 'outside' status and gendered context of their everyday lives meant that settlement and cultural adjustment was far from easy. For some of the young return migrants, kinship and friendship networks back in England provided invaluable support, particularly for the female participants who found it hard to establish friendships with the native-born women. Whilst others, aware of their problems that emerged from their 'outside' status, regarded return migration as a temporary measure born out of pragmatism and practical necessity, rather than a genuine commitment to building transnational family ties.

Acknowledgements

I would like to thank Russell King and Anastacia Christou at Sussex University's Centre of Migration Research (SCMR) for their encouragement and guidance in writing this article, and also their detailed feedback on earlier drafts of the working paper.

Notes

1. This category refers exclusively to the offspring of British-Caribbean migrants that migrate or 'return' to their parents' Caribbean country of origin. It is not within the scope of this article to critically interrogate the complexity and ambiguity of this concept, or indeed problematize the multiple ways the term has been used as both a descriptive and an analytic category. King and Christou's (2008) analysis concerning the conceptualizations of 'generations', particularly the term 'second generation', in migration studies provides a detailed review and critique of this issue.

2. Research undertaken within the Families and Social Capital ESRC Research Group (2003–2007) entitled 'Caribbean Young People, Social Capital and Diasporic Family Relationships' (Reynolds 2004). *This* research forms part of the Families and Social Capital ESRC Research Group programme of work (ESRC Award Reference: M570255001). Research undertaken at SCMR (2007) was entitled 'Caribbean Second Generation Return Migration', funded by London South Bank University.

3.   Most of the research into return migration to Jamaica has focused on the area of Mandeville in southern parish of Manchester, where there is an established resident and thriving returning resident community (Goubourne 2002; Horst 2005). I purposely chose not to use Mandeville as a research site for a number of reasons. This area is experiencing 'research fatigue' in terms of the number of studies emerging from the UK, the Caribbean, Canada and North America that have used this area to explore return migration (Goulbourne 2002). Furthermore, it is primarily dominated by *retired* returning migrants who had previously built up their economic capital in their migrant country of destination before returning to their country of origin.
4.   See www.lsbu.ac.uk/families.
5.   Colloquial Jamaican term used by native-born residents to identify individuals migrating or visiting from other countries.
6.   There were some differences to this according to urban-rural settings. Female participants who were unmarried, single and lived in the towns reported more spaces to socialize with their female friends (e.g. going to the cinema or gym) compared to the female participants who lived in rural areas, where social spaces outside of the home and work were very restricted for both married and single women.
7.   The challenges of gender-related expectations and practices in the Caribbean support earlier writings on the greater freedom that first generation female migrants experienced in Britain and the US (Foner 2005).

References

ABENATY, FRANK 2001 'The dynamics of return migration to St. Lucia', in H. Goulbourne and M. Chamberlain (eds), *Caribbean Families in Britain and the Transatlantic World*, London: Macmillan, pp. 170–187
ADAMS, REBECCA and ALLAN, GRAHAM (eds) 1998 *Placing Friendships in Context*, Cambridge: Cambridge University Press
BALDASSAR, LORETTA 2001 *Visits Home: Migration Experiences between Italy and Australia*, Melbourne: Melbourne University Press
BAUER, ELAINE and THOMPSON, PAUL 2006 *Jamaican Hands across the Atlantic*, Kingston: Ian Randle Publishers
BRYON, MARGARET 1999 'The Caribbean-born population in 1990s Britain: who will return?', *Journal of Ethnic and Migration Studies*, vol. 25, no. 2, pp. 285–301
BRYON, MARGARET 2000 'Return migration to the Eastern Caribbean: comparative experiences and policy implications', *Social and Economic Studies*, vol. 49, no. 9, pp. 155–89
CHAMBERLAIN, MARY 1997 *Narratives of Exile and Return*, London: Macmillan Press
CHAMBERLAIN, MARY 2006 *Family Love in the Diaspora: Migration and the Anglo-Caribbean Experience*, New Brunswick, NJ: Transaction Publishers
CHEUNG, SIN YI and HEATH, ANTHONY 2007 '"Nice work if you can get it": ethnic penalties in Great Britain', *Proceedings of the British Academy*, vol. 137, pp. 507–50
CHRISTOU, ANASTASIA 2006 'American dream and European nightmares: experiences and polemics of second generation Greek-American returning migrants', *Journal of Ethnic and Migration Studies*, vol. 32, no. 5, pp. 831–45
DUVAL, DAVID 2002 'The return visit – return migration connection', in C.M. Hall and A.M. Williams (eds), *Tourism and Migration*, Amsterdam: Kluwer Academic Publishers, pp. 257–276
EDWARDS, ROSALIND, FRANKLIN, JANE and HOLLAND, JANET 2003 'Families and Social Capital: Exploring the Issues', Families & Social Capital ESRC Research Group Working Paper Series, no. 1, London: South Bank University

FARLEY, REYNOLDS and RICHARD, ALBA 2002 'The new second generation in the United States', *International Migration Review*, vol. 36, no. 3, pp. 669–701

FOG-OLWIG, KAREN 2007 *Caribbean Journeys: An Ethnography of Migration and Home in Three Family Networks*, Durham, NC: Duke University Press

FONER, NANCY 2002 'Second generation transnationalism, then and now'', in P. Levitt and M. Waters (eds), *The Changing Face of Home: The Transnational Lives of the Second Generation*, New York: Russell Sage, pp. 459–479

FONER, NANCY 2005 *In A New Land*, New York: New York University Press

FRANKLIN, JANE 2007 'Social Capital: Between Harmony and Dissonance', Families & Social Capital ESRC Research Group Working Paper Series no. 18, London: South Bank University

GILBERT, NIGEL (eds), 1994 *Researching Social Life*, London: Sage

GLICK-SCHILLER, NINA 2004 'Transnationality', in D.Nugent and J. Vincent (eds), *A Companion to the Anthropology of Politics*, Malden, UK: Blackwell, pp. 46–47

GMELCH, GEORGE 1980 'Return migration', *Annual Review of Anthropology*, vol. 9, pp. 135–59

GMELCH, GEORGE 1992 *Double Passage: The Lives of Caribbean Migrants Abroad and Back Home*, Ann Arbor, MI: University of Michigan Press

GOULBOURNE, HARRY 2002 *Caribbean Transnational Experience*, London: Pluto Press

GOULBOURNE, HARRY, REYNOLDS, TRACEY, SOLOMOS, JOHN and ZONTINI, ELISABETTA Forthcoming *Transnational Families*, London: Routledge

GRILLO, RALPH 2008 'The family in dispute: insiders and outsiders', in R. Grillo (ed.), *The Family in Question: Immigration and Ethnic Minorities in Multicultural Europe*, Amsterdam: Amsterdam University Press

HEATH, ANTHONY 2008 'The second generation in Western Europe: education, unemployment and occupational attainment', *Annual Review of Sociology*, vol. 34, pp. 153–79

HORST, HEATHER 2005 'Landscaping Englishness: the post colonial predicament of returnees in Mandeville, Jamaica', in R.B. Potter, D. Conway and J. Phillips (eds), *The Experience of Return Migration: Caribbean Perspectives*, Aldershot, UK: Ashgate

KASINITZ, PHILLLIP, MOLLENKOPF, JOHN, WATERS, MARY and HOLDAWAY, JENNIFER 2008 *Inheriting the City: The Children of Immigrants Come of Age*, New York: Russell Sage Foundation

KING, RUSSELL 2000 'Generalizations from the history of return migration', in B. Ghosh (ed.), *Return Migration: Journey of Hope or Despair*, Geneva: International Organization for Migration and the United Nations

KING, RUSSELL and CHRISTOU, ANASTASIA 2008 'Cultural Geographies of Counter-Diasporic Migration Diaspora', SCMR Working Paper Series, University of Sussex

LEVITT, PEGGY 2001 *The Transnational Villagers*, Berkeley, CA: University of California Press

LEVITT, PEGGY and WATERS, MARY (eds) 2002 *The Changing Face of Home: The Transnational Lives of the Second Generation*, New York: Russell Sage

MORROW, VIRGINIA (ed) 2001 'Conceptualising social capital in relation to the well-being of children and young people: a critical review', *Sociological Review*, vol. 47, no. 4, pp. 744–65

OWEN, DAVID 2006 'Demographic profiles and social cohesion of minority ethnic communities in England and Wales, special issue: ethnicity and social capital', *Journal of Community, Work and Family*, vol. 9, no. 3, pp. 251–72

PAHL, RAY and PEVALIN, DAVID 2005 'Between family and friends: a longitudinal study of friendship choice', *The British Journal of Sociology*, vol. 56, no. 3, pp. 433–50

PHILLIPS, JOAN and POTTER, ROBERT 2005 'Incorporating race and gender into Caribbean return migration: the example of second generation "Bajan-Brits"', in R.B. Potter,

D. Conway and J. Phillips (eds), *The Experience of Return Migration: Caribbean Perspectives*, Aldershot, UK: Ashgate

PLANNING INSTITUTE OF JAMAICA 2004 *Economic and Social Survey Jamaica 2003*, Kingston: The Planning Institute of Jamaica

PLATT, LUCINDA 2005 'The intergenerational mobility of minority ethnic groups', *Sociology*, vol. 39, no. 3, pp. 445–61

PLAZA, DWAINE 2000 'In pursuit of the mobility dream: second generation British-Caribbeans returning to Jamaica and Barbados', *Journal of Eastern Caribbean Studies*, vol. 27, no. 4, pp. 135–60

POTTER, ROBERT B 2005 'The socio-demographic characteristics of second generation return migrants to St. Lucia and Barbados', in R. B. Potter, D. Conway and J. Phillips (eds), *The Experience of Return Migration: Caribbean Perspectives*, Aldershot, UK: Ashgate

POTTER, ROBERT B., CONWAY, DENNIS and PHILLIPS, JOAN (eds) 2005 *The Experience of Return Migration: Caribbean Perspectives*. Aldershot, UK: Ashgate

POTTER, ROBERT B. and PHILLIPS, JOAN 2006a 'Both black and symbolically white: the 'Bajan-Brit' return migrant as post-colonial hybrid', *Ethnic and Racial Studies*, vol. 29, no. 5, pp. 901–27

POTTER, ROBERT B. and PHILLIPS, JOAN 2006b '"Mad dogs and international migrants?" Bajan-Brit second generation migrants and accusation of madness', *Annals of the Association of American Geographies*, vol. 96, no. 3, pp. 586–600

PUTNAM, ROBERT 2000 *Bowling Alone – The Collapse and Revival of American Community*, New York: Simon & Schuster

PUTNAM, ROBERT 2007 'E Pluribus Unum: diversity and community in the twenty-first century; the 2006 Johan Skytte Prize Lecture', *Scandinavian Political Studies*, vol. 30, no. 2, pp. 137–74

REYNOLDS, TRACEY 2004 'Caribbean Families, Social Capital and Young People's Diasporic Identities', Families and Social Capital ESRC Research Group Working Paper Series, no. 12, London: South Bank University

REYNOLDS, TRACEY 2006a 'Caribbean young people, family relationships and social capital; special issue: social capital, migration and transnational families', *Journal of Ethnic and Racial Studies*, vol. 29, no. 6, pp. 1087–103

REYNOLDS, TRACEY 2006b 'Bonding social capital within the Caribbean family and community; special issue: ethnicity and social capital', *Journal of Community, Work and Family*, vol. 9, no. 3, pp. 273–90

REYNOLDS, TRACEY 2007 'Friendship networks, social capital and ethnic identity: researching the perspectives of Caribbean young people in Britain', *Journal of Youth Studies*, vol. 10, no. 4, pp. 383–98

SUTTON, CONSTANCE 2004 'Celebrating ourselves: the family rituals of African-Caribbean transnational families', *Global Networks: A Journal of Transnational Affairs*, vol. 4, no. 3, pp. 243–57

THOMAS-HOPE, ELIZABETH 1992 *Explanation in Caribbean Migration: Perception and the Image: Jamaica, Barbados and St. Vincent*, London: Macmillan

WATERS, MARY 1999 *Black Identities: West Indian Immigrants: Dreams and Realities*, Cambridge, MA: Harvard University Press

WESSENDORF, SUSANNE 2007 '"Roots migrants": transnationalism and "return" among second generation Italians in Switzerland', *Journal of Ethnic and Migration Studies*, vol. 33, no. 7, pp. 1083–102

WINTER, IAN 2002 'Towards a Theorised Understanding of Family and Social capital', Working Paper no. 21, Australian Institute of Family Studies

ZONTINI, ELISABETTA 2004 'Italian Families and Social Capital: Rituals and the Provision of Care in British-Italian Transnational Families', Families & Social Capital ESRC Research Group Working Paper, no. 6, London: South Bank University

Enabling and constraining aspects of social capital in migrant families: ethnicity, gender and generation

Elisabetta Zontini

Abstract

This article sets out to examine the use, production and maintenance of social capital in the context of migration through an in-depth analysis of the everyday experiences of young people in Italian families in the UK and Italy. Social capital is usually described in the literature as membership in networks that either helps individuals to get ahead or to preserve positions of power. In this article, I move beyond these one-sided understandings of social capital by exploring both the positive and negative traits of family and ethnic solidarity, as specific forms of social capital for Italian young people By focusing on the experiences of Italian young people, the analysis also demonstrates that gender and generation are crucial axes for interpreting different experiences in participating in strong family and ethnic networks.

Introduction

This article is about migrant Italian families and the tensions existing between creating and maintaining strong networks and the societal push towards, or the desire for, individualization. My analysis starts from debates around social capital since the role of networks, families and increasingly ethnicity play a significant part in them. However, as the article will show, I end up problematizing and somewhat departing from the concept, since I found that it fails to explain some of the causes for people's participation in strong networks and the consequences for the individuals who do so. Emotions, identities and values, I will argue, need to be included in social capital theory, since they might help explain the reasons why networks are created and maintained, as well as their consequences. Section one briefly introduces the study on which the article is based, whereas section two interrogates the social capital literature in the light of the interviews with Italians in the UK. The third section spells out the characteristics of the idealized Italian family as bedrock against which to compare the everyday experiences of my interviewees. The following two sections deal in turn with families and communities as sources of support and solidarity and with their darker side, looking at the kind of pain and conflicts they might generate.

The study

This article draws on the results of a three-year research project entitled Italian Families and Social Capital: Rituals and the Provision of Care in British Italian Families, which formed part of the Ethnicity Stand of the Families and Social Capital ESRC Research Group at South Bank University. Methodologically, the project consisted of participant observation and interviews in different sites with both men and women belonging to different generations. Given the assumption that family and ethnic social capital have both local and transnational dimensions, alongside fieldwork in the UK two case-studies were also conducted in two Italian towns of large emigration, one located in the north and one in the south. Drawing on the work of Di Leonardo (1984), the emphasis in constructing the sample was on diversity rather than homogeneity. Different groups of Italians were interviewed in order to include those belonging to the three main migration waves – pre-war, post-war and recent professional and student migration – and their offspring, and both northern and southern Italians. In the UK, fieldwork entailed conducting fifty interviews both in selected industrial towns of large Italian post-war immigration (Bedford, Peterborough and Aylesbury), and in London, where both pre-war migrants and recent professional migrants have settled. Interviews were conducted with people of different generations, ranging from teenagers to elderly people. Usually more than one member of the same family was interviewed and where possible this also included relatives residing in Italy (Zontini 2004a). Among those interviewed in the UK, nineteen were migrants' offspring born in the UK. Of these thirteen were female and five were male. Although not all of them were 'young' at the time of interview (their ages ranged from sixteen to sixty-seven, with the majority in the late thirties), they all reflected on what it meant to be young in Italian families and on their experiences of growing up as children of migrants. In this article, I use some of the extracts of the interviews with the younger of them to interrogate the social capital literature and to reflect on the tensions between networks and societal pushes or desire for individualization.

Deeper engagement with the life histories and biographies of my interviews can be found elsewhere, as are some reflections on methodology, positionality and access (Zontini 2004c, 2006, 2007). In the project, social capital and ethnicity were not seen as properties that can be clearly defined and measured. Migrants' identities, networks and social capital were understood within the context of specific geographic and symbolic locales, rather than in abstract and as fluid properties that get reformulated in the process of everyday life in the homeland and in the host country (Evergeti and Zontini 2006).

Social capital and Italian families

Social capital is usually described in the literature as membership in networks that either helps individuals to get ahead or, drawing on the work of Bourdieu (1997), helps them to preserve positions of power. For Coleman (1990), social capital is generated in the family because it produces high levels of obligations and expectations. It also provides information potential, and generates norms and effective sanctions. Arguing from a very different theoretical position, Bourdieu (1997) draws the attention 'on the strategies individuals employ as they invest in and capitalise on social, economic and cultural resource' (Franklin 2007, p. 3). Similarly to Coleman, however, he too sees families as sources of social capital used to preserve positions of power and thus perpetuating social inequalities.

Alongside the family, ethnicity has also started to be seen as a form of social capital, especially in the US sociological literature, which is preoccupied with understanding processes of adaptation of the so-called second generation (Zhou 1992; Portes and Zhou 1993; Zhou and Bankston 1994; Portes and Rumbaut 2001). This literature maintains that different ethnic groups draw upon family, kinship and communal resources with different degrees of success (Zontini and Reynolds 2007; Shah 2007). Ethnicity as social capital as been seen as a factor that helps social mobility (Modood 2004). There is thus an underlying assumption in part of the academic literature, as well as in the policy literature that has embraced the concept, that social capital is positive, since it allows people to mobilize collective resources for personal benefit.

These functionalist definitions and understandings of social capital do not fit easily with my material on Italian families. People of Italian origin are enmeshed in a variety of networks based on kin or ethnic relations that are characterized by the kind of closure, presence of trust and maintenance of strict norms and values advocated by Coleman. Yet, as Anthias (2007) rightly highlights, such networks are not necessarily mobilizable for pursuing advantage. Nor are competitive and hierarchical concerns necessarily what motivates my interviewees (Karner and Parker 2008). They did not regard their participation in networks and reciprocal exchanges of resources as merely means for personal advancement, nor were they used to preserve positions of power.

Edwards and Gillies (2005) note that working class families more generally participate in dense networks of family and friends. The strong emotional bonds they have with each other are expressed as interdependency, obligation and commitment rather than a means for personal gain. The difference in my study is that the young Italian people's participation in dense networks is not merely a necessity for survival, since the majority of people in my sample are now economically secure. What emerges in my interviews is that solidarity and cooperation among kin (and to some extent among *paesani* – people of the same village – and co-ethnics) are important values for them. They are crucial traits of young Italian people's identity, and underpinned by norms that, although changing, are still strongly felt.

Francesca, for instance, talks about helping family and community members as a trait of her Italian identity:

> It's a very positive thing that I'm able to not be completely selfish. I remember when my father went into hospital some people were saying "Why do you have to go every time?" For me it would be bad not to go. *This is very Italian* that yourself is part of an extension of something very bigger like THE FAMILY. (Francesca, 36, academic, interview site: London)

Idealized Italian families

In order to understand the nature and the values associated with participating in strong networks and reciprocal exchanges, it is important to understand the context in which they emerge. Of importance here is the distinction made by Williams (2004) between the normative family and the lived experiences of family lives. The normative family is what people aspire to, the ideal that guides their behaviour. For migrants, such a family ideal might be constructed in dialogue and sometimes in opposition to what they perceive to be 'the family' for the majority population. Migrants may use family practices as a way to draw boundaries between them and the majority population (Charles, Aull Davies and Harris 2008).

In order to understand the kind of social capital operating in Italian families, I therefore think that it is important to spell out what seem to be some of the values underpinning it as they emerged in my fieldwork. I will therefore start with a brief analysis of the young people's views of Italian families by highlighting the idealized image of Italian families.

In my interviews, three specific traits emerged as important facets of Italian families (irrespective of whether these matched their lived experience) and which Italian people felt differentiated them from other families in the UK. They were cooperation, togetherness and strong intergenerational connections – all featuring also in social capital discourse. The first element that emerged as important was cooperation. As other authors have noted, Italian families can be seen as cooperative units united through reciprocal rights and obligations. These relationships have to be seen as pervasive and implicit rather than definite and explicit (Sturino 1980). The assumption that family should be there to support is clear in many of the interviews I conducted.

The second element that should characterize Italian families is togetherness (by which is meant living close and seeing each other often). Dario, for instance, explains how always being together is an important characteristic of Italian families:

> I think what I found when I was growing up is that I was always round my cousin's house whereas my friends were never with their families. They were only with their family on special occasions, so in that respect it was definitely Italian, like on the *Godfather*, you're one big family and you're always together, sometimes you didn't want to if it was an old aunt and you just sit there and get bored but you just do it! (Dario, 28, business owner, interview site: London)

Reflecting the quotation above, the third element that should constitute an Italian family is strong intergenerational relations. Adult children should visit their parents often and do small favours for them. When they become frail, it is the children's responsibility (usually women) to look after them, ideally at home. Parents for their part are expected to provide economically for their children well into adulthood. They will normally pay for their marriages and buy or help put down a deposit for their first house. These are the traits that my interviewees felt were defining Italian families, and this was the ideal against which they judged their own and other people's behaviour.

Young adults and Italian families: the positive side of social capital

My study of Italian families found that in many respect they matched the ideal Italian family, performing numerous emotional and practical tasks. The families studied generated within them both bonding and bridging forms of social capital (Putnam 2000). For instance, as well as strengthening bonds derived by sharing an ethnic origin, these families bridged differences of gender, generation, language, nationality, ethnicity, class, place of residence and region of origin. The research found that even if people of Italian origin became separated through migration, they were still enmeshed in a complex web of relationships linking them to wider kin groups located in a variety of geographical contexts and to their wider communities in Italy, the UK and elsewhere. As scholars of migration and transnationalism have demonstrated, social capital cannot be seen as exclusively locality-based (Gupta and Ferguson 1992; Levit 2001; Bryceson and Vourela 2002). Transnational communities create networks of trust and reciprocity across geographical neighbourhoods and nation states.

As is the case for many migrant groups, maintaining these transnational relationships – 'caring about' or 'kin work' in Di Leonardo's (1992) terminology – were crucial for my Italian interviewees, and they devoted time and energy to this (Zontini 2006, Reynolds and Zontini 2006). Frequent and regular telephone conversations are an important way to keep families together, updating scattered members about what is going on in each others' lives, providing emotional support and even directing and organising more hands on care from other family members. Family rituals also play an important function in bringing distant family members together and reaffirming continuity – they range from the everyday (such as the family meal), to cyclical (such as Christmas dinners), to life-cycle (the major one being the wedding). However, the most important way in which kin connections are kept for both migrants and their offspring is the frequent visit 'home', which, in both practical and symbolic dimensions, bring together scattered members while also confirming migrants' commitment to their roots and kin left behind (Baldassar 2001). All of my interviewees, irrespective of age, generation or economic situation, were involved in visiting with a frequency that ranged from monthly to at least once a year.

Marta, for instance, who was born in the UK, has always visited Italy every year. Even her work choices in the UK were related to her need to spend some time in Italy and to her other life there:

I used to work for 11 months and then go to Italy for a month, and then come back and get another job. All the friends are up there [Italy], all the cousins are up there for the holidays. (Marta, local authority employee, interview site: London)

In the case of Marta, the Italian 'connection' has been transmitted to her children – third generation Italians – thus showing how transnationalism perpetuates itself in families, albeit in different forms (Baldassar 2001, Panagakos 2004). Talking about her children's visits she says:

They all want to go. They like it up there, they love the food. They like being Italian, cos you know fashion and football, and motorbikes, all the best bikes are Italian, style. They want to learn Italian so I brought them a CD for beginners, it's very nice it's all 'Buongiorno', they know all that ...

Being part of strong networks, both local and transnational, also has very concrete benefits, allowing members to access resources circulating in them. The research found that care is one of the main resources circulating in the families studied both locally and transnationally. Intergenerational care and support emerged as particularly strong. Children are an important part of the aged networks of support, for instance helping with translations, form-filling, domestic work, emotional support, and so on. All of the migrants' offspring interviewed (both males and females) reported playing a key role in their parents everyday life, both now that they are elderly and throughout their life. Paolo, talking of when he was growing up:

> We started integrating speaking English and then obviously if they ever needed to go anywhere we would always have to go with them. Me being the oldest, if my parents had to go to a Doctor or to the Hospital or to do anything and sometimes even to the shops, I would have to go with them and interpret what was going on. (Paolo, 38, bar owner, interview site: Bedford)

Even now, his elderly parents as well as his in-laws are rarely left on their own. Paolo and his wife visit them regularly several times a week, they drive them to do the shopping and to doctors' appointments, and include them in all family celebrations.

Elderly Italian migrants, however, are not just recipients of support; they are often important providers as well. 'Flying Grandmas' (Reynolds and Zontini 2006) move from the UK to Italy or the other way around to support their children with babysitting and being involved in their grandchildren upbringing. They also help their children if they live locally, changing their holidays or even their retirement plans if they are needed in the UK. The migrants' offspring know that they can generally rely on their parents (especially mothers) for support. Marcella, for instance, was helped by her mother when she divorced her Italian husband and came back to the UK with two young children:

> I came back to my Mother ... she said we'll live together and it was the best thing that could have happened to me and my children because I was able to go to work and so I could support them ... I was able to afford all the classes ... the swimming and the clarinet and everything because I was with my Mum and I didn't have to pay rent and if I ever wanted to go out in the evening I knew the children were at home. (Marcella, 39, secretary, interview site: London)

This section has briefly shown how the family represents an important source of care and support for young and elderly Italians alike, matching in many respects the ideal Italian family described previously, as well as the virtuous family depicted in the social capital literature (Coleman 1990). I now turn to the flip-side of families and communities, focusing on their more problematic aspects.

The negative side of family and ethnic social capital

A critique of the social capital literature is that it tends to emphasize the positive sides of strong networks, idealize the cooperative nature of some ethnic groups and, in so doing, to overlook power relations within groups (Portes 1998). Feminist scholars have drawn attention to power relations within families and groups, especially along gender and generational lines (Oakely 1974, Anthias and Yuval-Davies 1992). Following Portes (1998) and Molyneaux (2001), I have argued elsewhere (Zontini 2004b, 2006) that social capital is not necessarily positive for everyone all the time. For example, as emerged from the previous section, women may have a crucial role for the creation and maintenance of social capital. The kind of kin and caring work which Italian families carry out is predominately, although not exclusively, women's work (Di Leonardo 1992). Such work, as I will show, may be experienced by some of them as an unwanted burden (Zontini, 2002).

Feminists (e.g. Oakely 1974) and other theorists (e.g. Bourdieu 1997) have long drown attention to the power struggles that go on in families, but little attention has so far been given to the centrality of emotions for understanding families and relationships (Smart 2007). As many feminist authors have shown (Smart 2007; Charles, Aull Davies and Harris 2008), all relationships are not cancellable as argued by promoters of the individualization thesis (Giddens 1992; Beck and Beck-Gernsheim 2002; Bauman 2003). Individuals are involved in negotiating ties and responsibilities rather than simply breaking away from difficult relationships. Smart (2007) has started to draw attention to the darker side of the families we live with, focusing on the experiences of living with ongoing difficult relationships. Feelings that she explores are anxiety, hurt and lack of respect, which are common in our everyday family living. In her view, the feeling of anxiety might be particularly acute in immigrant families due to the insecurity provoked by migrants' marginal position in the receiving society. When looking at Italian immigrant families, issues connected to shame and respectability (Skeggs 1997), or to honour and shame as they are termed in the anthropological literature (Sciama 2003), might be equally relevant. Smart addresses feelings of hurt and distress in the context of parents–children relationships in post-divorce families. My work, as well as that of Edwards and Gillies (2005), has focused instead on the pain provoked by broken expectations. For Smart, disrespect is the result of unequal power relationships within families which might result in weaker members being ignored, disregarded or neglected. These feelings were often experienced by the young women living in some of the partriarchal households I have studied. Disrespect was also experienced in relation to the provision of support. Some authors have started to point out that emotional support in families is not without strings, in spite of the rhetoric of the opposite. Especially in Italian families, support can be used to shape behaviour and strongly associated with control. Another important feeling present in several of the interviews was the issue of guilt.

Some of the negative feelings reported to me originated from families trying to cling to particular family and cultural practices. Often such practices reinforced gender and generational divisions (Anthias and Yuval-Davies 1992; Shah 2007) and were seen by some family members as oppressive. Examples of this in the Italian context had to do with dissatisfaction around the gendered division of work inside and outside the household and with issues to do with freedom and control.

Marta recalled how she divorced her husband because he was expecting her to do everything. She explains:

Well his mum used to wash his back and put his clothes on his bed that he was going to be wearing that night and they were served hand and foot in this family you know. I should have known then, I should have seen it, but I said to Gino you know I'm not like your mother, I said, you know *I'm not like an Italian woman*, I'm not going to serve you? He expected me to be his mother. He wouldn't do anything, nothing at all, at all. (Marta, local authority employee, interview site: London)

Worth noticing is that Marta interprets wishing for a fairer division of domestic work as being 'un-Italian'. Marta did not put up with her unhappy marriage and left her husband, but this was not without consequences. Her family did not approve of her decision, which they thought would bring shame on their family. Given that it was Marta who initiated the divorce and that her reasons for doing so were seen by others as well as herself as her refusal to be 'a proper Italian woman', her family sided with her son-in- law rather than with her. She was forced out of the top flat in her parents' house, while her ex-husband continued to live there.

Many respondents (mostly young women) felt that their families' protection and support was often a double-edged sword. Women talked about strong emotional bonds of dependency that, in their view, were at times abused by some family members. Marta, as other interviewees in my larger sample, talks about this in terms of 'emotional blackmail'. Here is an example she gives:

And I remember I phoned my mum once, from Italy, to see how everything was, and she talked to me and she said: "oh your dad's ill", my dad was never ill you know, and "it's all your fault", I was like "oh thank you!" ... Emotional blackmail was terrible, and because my brother died in India and then my other brother went to America at the same time, I couldn't do anything [she would say:] "oh if you go I'll be all on my own" and "you don't care if I die". When she died, it's a horrible thing to say, but I felt relief, I felt so free, so free.

As mentioned earlier, interviewees talked about how support is linked to the fact that the receiver is expected to subscribe to certain norms and values. Laura – who is a PA born in Italy and now in her early forties – felt that those giving support want to influence the choices of those receiving it and that support is linked to obligations. Gabriella – a UK-born teacher in her late thirties – says that this is the reason why she never relies on family when she needs support. For her, support means subscribing to her father's values and she refuses to do that. She is envious of the kind of unconditional support that she assumes exist in other Italian families.

In contrast to the ideal of family togetherness, unity and coopera-tion many young people (especially women) felt neglected as children. This has stark resemblance with the narratives of the children of transnational families studied by Parrenas (2005), who also talk about the inadequacy of care they received in their families. What is interesting is that, in both studies, children talk about the lack of care received from their mothers while rarely blaming their fathers, even though they worked just as hard. Parrenas explains this in the context of gender boundaries. Fathers, she argues, are expected by their gender role to be providers, whereas mothers, especially in the Italian ideal, are expected to be primarily nurturers. Another issue that is recurrent in the interviews with young British-Italian women is the burden they felt in having to look after themselves from a very young age. All talk about returning home from school to empty houses, having to cook their own meals or even that of their fathers, and having to take up part of their mothers' share of housework (their brothers and fathers were exempt from this and many of my interviewees resented this). Many resented the responsibilities and independence that were forced upon them (Parrenas 2005).

Their feelings, however, have to be interpreted in relation to the experience of their parents, low-paid workers in a little known and often hostile environment. Pressures resulting from the difficulties of making ends meet (especially in the early migration years) and the kind of anxiety resulting from the worries associated with living in a new environment, might in some cases have resulted in a difficult family environment. In such contexts, parents tried to adhere to what was known to them in terms of family practices (strict gender and generational norms) – thus at times exacerbating conflicts with their children (Shah 2007).

Although some problems were caused by families adherence to so-called 'traditional' family values, many of the emotional problems I encountered had a different cause, namely the mismatch between the ideal family and the reality of everyday family life. Feeling hurt was often the result of broken expectations, especially around the three elements sustaining the ideal Italian family reported above. The feeling of rupture caused by unmet expectations was found to be common in the dense social networks of the working class families studied by Edwards and Gillies (2005). This was also found in the Italian case study. The case of Donatella's family is particularly interesting in this context, because it shows how different values that underpinned the idealized Italian family can actually clash against each other. Individuals are often not clear what to do because obligations are pervasive and implicit (rather than explicit), leading to different family members having conflicting expectations.

In Donatella's family, her married sister now lives in Italy, near to where her parents have decided to retire (they were formerly migrant workers in the UK). Her sister expected that, because they were retired, they would have looked after her children while she worked. Her parents, however, believed that it was the younger generation that had the duty to support the older one. When they retired after years of hard work in London, they were shocked to discover that their daughter expected them to look after her young children. According to Donatella, this clash of expectations brought many conflicts in her family and is an issue still not resolved.

Another typical example of broken expectations characterizes the experience of several first-generation migrant workers, and it emerged particularly from my fieldwork in Sicily. This is the failure of having accomplished family togetherness in spite of all the *sacrifici* (sacrifices) undertaken to this end. This explains why young British-Italian people (especially women) feel compelled to live close to their parents. Those who had done so at times expressed regret for not having fulfilled their ambitions, whereas those who had moved away from family had to live with the constant feeling of guilt. In Gabriella's words: 'for years I just went around feeling guilty about being happy.'

Control and pressure to conform to strict norms emerged as the flip side of family and ethnic solidarity. This emerged as particularly acutely in the large close-knit Italian communities of post-war migration in the industrial towns of Bedford and Peterborough but which I found in looser forms also elsewhere. Here, rigid norms and values are maintained and people (especially women) have either to comply or find their way out (but this came at high price for my interviewees). Below is just one example:

I was very interested in books and the community is very old fashioned and very narrow minded. They tried to bring up their children in the only way they knew which was very Catholic and very old fashioned and narrow. They didn't value education unlike other immigrant communities, they didn't value education and they certainly didn't value it for me as a daughter. Not just my parents, I mean the community ... the aspirations within the community is that you would just get married as quickly as possible within the community ...

And for me books were my kind of salvation really and I was drawing and doing poetry but books particularly ... It was very difficult. My mother was quite supportive, my father not at all. ... He left school when he was 9 and he had no idea ... he equated reading with being lazy so I had huge arguments and I should go and help my mother in the kitchen rather than sit around reading. I know this is very much linked with the class ... he wasn't very literate himself and there weren't any books in my house until I brought them in so ...

I think it was quite hard for my parents to come to terms with me to have quite different aspirations and that I wasn't interested in being married or going out with the local Italian who was deemed a good catch so ... It was very hard for them, very hard because as I said, the community is very old fashioned so my parents really suffered ... because my brother and I left at the same time to go to university and they were left there having to deal with people's prejudices and ignorance and it was very hard...

They thought my father's masculinity had been tainted or damaged and they thought that I should never be allowed back home. It was very old fashioned and previously you see, because my mother was a dressmaker for the community I was the perfect daughter and I spoke perfect Italian and I would read their letters for them ... so I went from having quite a particular role within the community and then to leave home was transgressing everything. God, it was very difficult in the beginning. I remember some of them when I went back to visit, they would cross the road and pretend not to see me and very prejudiced and very old fashioned about ... so leaving home was like going to be a prostitute ...

London is different ... people move in and moved around ... and they don't have the pressure of that stability of what the community was in the way that I did. I had some close friends of mine who were brought up in Kettering and they were the only Italian family ... I was always struck by the fact that they didn't have those pressures. So for example they all went to university and it wasn't a big deal and two of them married Englishmen. I think it was because they didn't have the pressures of codes of conduct within the community and how they think things had to be. (Francesca, 36, academic, interview site: London).

The story of Francesca shows that, as many feminist scholars have pointed out, escaping families and communities is not as easy as proponents of the individualization theory seem to suggest (Smart 2007; Charles, Aull Davies and Harris 2008). People are enmeshed in complex networks where solidarity, responsibility and commitment operate. This does not mean that my respondents had no agency and passively accepted and endured the difficult relationships that I have just described. In the case of Francesca, her escape was through education. Other women in the study tried to escape from families and communities control through 'return' migration, although with very limited results (Wessendorf 2007; Zontini 2008). Others did manage to break away from unsatisfactory relationships, but that seemed easier when such relationships were with partners rather than with parents.

Conclusion

My research shows that emotions, identities and values are important in understanding the generation and maintenance of social capital. People of Italian origin participate in dense networks of family, kin and co-ethnics characterized by interdependency, obligation and commitment (not personal gain) that are similar to other British working class families such as those studied by Edwards and Gillies (2005). However, for British-Italians, participation in these networks is more than just a way to mitigate disadvantage (Anthias 2007), and this is the case for many other ethnic minority families (Evergeti 2006, Christou 2006). Notions of solidarity, reciprocity and cooperation are crucial values that are at the heart of people of Italian origin's identity. These values are used as markers of differentiation between Italians and the perceived amoral British population, and serve to reaffirm their belonging to families and communities. As feminist authors have argued against proponents of the individualization thesis, escaping from families is difficult and, looking at the experiences of my interviewees, rarely done. Belonging to families and communities was seen as crucial by my study participants, despite the tensions and conflict that this often generates. Family and ethnic social capital was rarely mobilized by women to obtain economic advantage, rather their efforts were dedicated to the accumulation or preservation of cultural and symbolic resources that reinforced their belonging to families and communities.

Participation in these strong networks emerged as having both positive and negative implications for the individuals involved. On the positive side, families were found to be resilient units providing numerous emotional and practical tasks in spite of geographical separation (many families seemed to match in many respects the ideal Italian family). On the negative side, I documented pain and conflicts brought about by broken expectations – often accompanied by feelings of guilt and regret – as well as how strong ethnic groups can preserve community cohesion and shared norms at the expense of the individuals in them.

The examples I have presented show, in my view, the importance of considering the complexity of family and ethnic social capital, which has positive as well as negative traits that are strongly interlinked and difficult to separate. They often co-exist side by side in the same families/communities, and can be interpreted in different ways depending on the point of view of different family members. Even if families can be seen as a locus of social capital of different forms, they need not be idealized. Participation in family networks requires considerable efforts, time and energy. Maintaining family connections and fulfilling family obligations both constrains and empowers the individuals involved in them, especially women who tend to do a bigger share of this type of work. This is why families are described by my interviewees both as sources of satisfaction, resources and benefits, but also of sorrow, tension and frustrations. This is why I believe that policy-makers who increasingly subscribe to a social capital discourse should be aware of its different dimensions and of the costs that relying on it can have for the individuals, families and communities involved.

Acknowledgements

This paper is based on material collected as part of a project conducted for the Families and Social Capital ESRC Research Group (see http://www.lsbu.ac.uk/families). I wish to thank Tracey Reynolds and the anonymous referees of this journal for their comments and suggestions.

References

ANTHIAS, F. 2007 'Ethnic ties: social capital and the question of mobilisability', *The Sociological Review*, vol. 55, no. 4, pp. 788–805

ANTHIAS, F. and YUVAL-DAVIS, N. 1992 *Racialised Boundaries: Race, Nation, Gender, Colour, and Class and the Anti-Racists Struggle*, London: Routledge

BALDASSAR, L. 2001 *Visits Home: Migration Experiences between Italy and Australia*, Melbourne: Melbourne University Press

BAUMAN, Z. 2003 *Liquid Love: On the Frailty of Human Bonds*, Cambridge: Polity Press

BECK, U. and BECK-GERNSHEIM, E. 2002 *Individualisation*, London: Sage

BOURDIEU, P. 1997 'The forms of capital', In: A. H. Halsey, H. Lauder, P. Brown and A.S. Wells (eds), *Education: Culture, Economy, Society*, Oxford: Oxford University Press, pp. 46–58

BRYCESON, D and VOURELA 2002 *The Transnational Family: New European Frontiers and Global Networks*, Oxford: Berg

CHARLES, N., AULL DAVIES, C. and HARRIS, C. 2008 *Families in Transition. Social Change, Family Formation and Kin Relationships*, Bristol, UK: Policy Press

CHRISTOU, A. 2006 'Deciphering diaspora – translating transnationalism: family dynamics, identity constructions and the legacy of "home" in second-generation Greek-American return migration', *Ethnic and Racial Studies*, vol. 29, no. 6, pp. 1040–1056

COLEMAN, J. S. 1990 *Foundations of Social Theory*, London: Harvard University Press

DI LEONARDO, M. 1984 *The Varieties of Ethnic Experience. Kinship, Class, and Gender among California Italian-Americans*, Ithaca: Cornell University Press

—— 1992 'The female world of cards and holidays: women, families and the work of kinship', in B. Thorne with M. Yalom (eds), *Rethinking the Family: Some Feminist Questions*, Boston, MA: Northern University Press, pp. 246–261

EDWARDS, R. and GILLIES, V. 2005 'Resources in Parenting: Access to Capitals Project Report', Working Article, no. 14, Families & Social Capital ESRC Research Group, London: London South Bank University

EVERGETI, V. 2006 'Living and caring between two cultures: narratives of Greek women in Britain', *Community Work and Family*, vol. 9, no. 3, pp. 347–66

EVERGETI, V. and ZONTINI, E. 2006 'Social capital, migration and transnational families: some critical reflections', *Ethnic and Racial Studies*, vol. 29, no. 6, pp. 1025–39

FRANKLIN, J. 2007 'Social capital: between harmony and dissonance', Working Paper no. 22, Families & Social Capital ESRC Research Group, London: London South Bank University

GIDDENS, A. 1992 *The Transformation of Intimacy: Sexuality, Love and Eroticism in Modern Societies*, Stanford: Stanford University Press

GUPTA, A. and FERGUSON, J. 1992 'Beyond "culture": space, identity, and the politics of difference', *Cultural Anthropology*, vol. 7, pp. 222–37

KARNER, K. and PARKER, D. 2008 'Religion versus rubbish: deprivation and social capital in inner-city Birmingham', *Social Compass*, vol. 55, no. 4, pp. 517–31

LEVITT, P. 2001 *The Transnational Villages*, Berkeley, CA: University of California Press

MODOOD, T. 2004 'Capitals, ethnic identity and educational qualifications', *Cultural Trends*, vol. 13, no. 2, pp. 87–105

MOLYNEAUX, M. 2001 'Social capital: a post transition concept? Questions of context and gender from Latin American perspective', in V. Morrow (ed.), *An Appropriate Capital-isation? Questioning Social Capital*, Research in Progress Series, Issue 1, Special Issue, Gender Institute, London School of Economics

OAKLEY, A. 1974 *The Sociology of Housework*, Oxford: Martin Robertson

PANAGAKOS, A. 2004 'Recycled odyssey: creating transnational families in the Greek diaspora', *Global Networks*, vol. 4, no. 3, pp. 299–311

PARREÑAS, R.S. 2001 *Servants of Globalization. Women, Migration, and Domestic Work*, Stanford, CA: Stanford University Press

—— 2005 *Children of Global Migration: Transnational Families and Gendered Woes*, Stanford University Press

PORTES, A. 1998 'Social capital: its origin and applications in modern sociology', *Annual Review of Sociology*, vol. 24, no. 1, pp. 1–24

PORTES, A. and RUMBAUT, R. 2001 *Legacies. The Story Of The Immigrant Second Generation*, Berkeley, CA: University of California Press

PORTES, A. and ZHOU, M. 1993 'The new second generation: segmented assimilation and its variants among post-1965 immigrant youth', *Annals of the American Academy of Political and Social Science*, vol. 530, pp. 74–98

PUTNAM, R. 2000 *Bowling Alone – The Collapse and Revival of American Community*, New York: Simon & Schuster

REYNOLDS, T. and ZONTINI, E. 2006 'A comparative study of care and provision across Caribbean and Italian transnational families', Working Article, no. 16, Families & Social Capital ESRC Research Group, London: London South Bank University

SCIAMA, L. 2003 *'A Venetian Island. Environment, History and Change in Burano*, Oxford: Berghahn Books

SHAH, B. 2007 'Being young, female and Laotian: ethnicity as social capital at the intersection of gender, generation, "race" and age', *Ethnic and Racial Studies*, vol. 30, no. 1, pp. 28–50

SKEGGS, B. 1997 *Formations of Class and Gender*, London: Sage

SMART, C. 2007 *Personal Life*, Cambridge: Polity Press

Wessendorf, S. 2007 '"Roots migrants": transnationalism and "return" among second-generation Italians in Switzerland', *The Journal of Ethnic and Migration Studies*, vol.33 no. 7 pp. 1083–102

STURINO, F. 1980 'Family and kin cohesion among Southern Italian immigrants in Toronto' in K. Ishweran (ed.) *Canadian Families: Ethnic Variatians*, Toronto: McGraw Hill Ryerson

WILLIAMS, F. 2004 *Rethinking Families*, London: Calouste Gulbenkian Foundation

ZHOU, M. 1992 *Chinatown: The Socioeconomic Potential of an Urban Enclave*, Philadelphia, PA: Temple University Press

ZHOU, M. and BANKSTON, C. 1994 'Social capital and the adaptation of the second generation: the case of Vietnamese Youth in New Orleans', *International Migration Review*, vol. 28, no. 4, pp. 821–45

ZONTINI, E. 2002 'Family Formation and Gendered Migrations in Bologna and Barcelona. A Comparative Ethnographic Study', DPhil thesis, University of Sussex

—— 2004a 'Immigrant women in Barcelona: coping with the consequences of transnational lives', *Journal of Ethnic and Migration Studies*, vol. 30, no. 6, pp. 1113–44

—— 2004b 'Italian families and social capital: rituals and the provision of care in British-Italian transnational families', Working Article, no. 6, Families & Social Capital ESRC Research Group, London: London South Bank University

—— 2004c 'Deploying social capital in social research: reflections on ethnicity and other resources' in R. Edwards (ed.), Working Paper no. 10, Social Capital in the Field, Families & Social Capital ESRC Research Group, London: London South Bank University [ISBN 1-8744418-46-2]

—— 2006 'Italian families and social capital: care provision in a transnational world', *Community, Work and Family*, vol. 9, no. 3, pp. 325–345

—— 2007 'Continuities and change in transnational Italian families: the caring practices of second generation women', *Journal of Ethnic and Migration Studies*, vol. 33, no. 7, pp. 1103–19

—— 2008 'Dreaming of "home" and "belonging" in transnational families: generational views on "return"', Paper presented at the 10th EASA Biennial Conference in Ljubljana, 26–30 August

ZONTINI, E. and REYNOLDS, T. 2007 'Ethnicity, families and social capital: caring relationships across Italian and Caribbean transnational families', *International Review of Sociology*, vol. 33, no. 7, pp. 1103–19

Care leavers and social capital: understanding and negotiating racial and ethnic identity

Ravinder Barn

Abstract

Young people leaving state care are recognized to be one of the most marginalized groups in society. In comparison to their counterparts living in their own family and community context, care leavers experience enormous adversity and upheaval. A combination of poor pre-care, in-care and post-care experiences serves to disadvantage this group of young people in many important ways. Moreover, research evidence documents the complexity of identity issues and concerns for minority ethnic children and young people who are separated from their birth families and are being brought up in public care. By drawing upon a recent and wider empirical study into care leavers in England, this paper explores the sociological concept of social capital and the ways in which this may contribute to young people's understanding and negotiation of their own racial and ethnic identity.

Introduction

There is considerable and growing interest, both nationally and internationally, in social capital and young people. Government policy in the UK is particularly concerned about building social capital to promote youth transitions to adult life, and to prevent problems such as poverty, homelessness, substance misuse and criminal activity among young people. Although there has been some recent attention focused on young people living within their own families and community, we know little about the social capital of young people in and leaving care (Armstrong 2002; Catan 2004).

There are about 60,000 children and young people looked after by the state in England (DCSF 2007). On average, about 8,000 young people leave the care system every year, many around the age of 17. Research evidence over the last several decades and now the government's own statistics indicate the disproportionate rates of some minority ethnic children and young people among those in care, and leaving care (Barn 2006; DCSF 2007).

Empirical research over the last several decades has documented poor outcomes for the majority of these children and young people, from all ethnic backgrounds. Compared to their counterparts in the general population, young people who have grown up in care are more likely to have poorer educational outcomes, and less likely to be engaged in post-16 education, they experience higher levels of unemployment, homelessness, mental health problems, and young parenthood, and they are more likely to be found engaged in risky behaviours including substance misuse, and offending behaviour (Biehal and Wade 1996; Broad 1999; Wade 2003; Barn, Andrew and Mantovani 2005; Stein 2006).

Thus, there is a substantial body of British and international literature on the impact and outcomes of state care for young people leaving care. Much of this literature attests to the state being an extremely wanting corporate parent. Amidst this body of work, there are three principal areas of concern. First, research evidence tells us of the poor pre-care experiences of many young people, which can include neglect, and physical, emotional and sexual abuse. Second, we know that the state as a corporate parent fails to adequately address the poor pre-care experiences, and may inadvertantly contribute to the path to social exclusion in its inability to offer stability and good care and guidance. Third, there are concerns about the transition of care leavers from care to the community, and from dependence to independence. Many care leavers are expected to make these transitions earlier than most other young people, and do not have the reassurance of falling back on their family if things do not work out (Jones 1995).

Young people living with their own families are arguably being raised in the 'safety net' of their support network system of family, friends, and the community. Such an environment is not only unavailable to the majority of care leavers, they also experience a great deal of instability in family placements, school settings, and geographical upheaval whilst in care. Such a precarious upbringing hampers emotional ties, and leads to a sense of uprootedness and lack of belonging. For children and young people who are defined as the 'other', absence of a supportive environment can result in questions about their location in a racialized society.

There is evidence to suggest that in addition to social exclusion and marginalization, concern has been expressed about the ways in which some minority ethnic young people in care struggle to make sense of their racial and ethnic identity in a racialized society (Banks 1992; Tizard and Phoenix 1993; Barn 1999; Robinson 2000; Barn and Harman 2006).

Racial and ethnic identity

During the phase of adolescence, racial and ethnic identity can be expected to constitute a significant phase of development, particularly for minority ethnic young people in the context of western contemporary multi-racial societies. Indeed, there is ongoing debate among academics, and practitioners, about the complexities of identity development for such youngsters. Evidence from some British studies suggests that 'ordinary', minority ethnic young people living with their own families do not generally experience problems and concerns about their racial and ethnic identity development (Tizard and Phoenix 1993; Fatimilehin 2002; Reynolds 2006). However, there is conflicting evidence regarding the identity development of minority ethnic young people in care and leaving care (First Key 1987; Ince 1998; Robinson 2000; Barn 2001). Concern is expressed about potential risk factors which may lead some young people to internalize racism and be ill-equipped to develop a positive racial and ethnic identity.

The terms race and ethnicity are often, mistakenly, used interchangeably to mean the same thing. Writers in the field of social science make important distinctions. Whilst 'race' is discredited as a biological term, and is generally understood to be a social construct to understand the dynamics of racism, ethnicity is often defined 'as denoting socio-cultural factors such as shared histories, memories, myths, customs, sentiments and values' (Goulbourne and Solomos 2003).

Racial and ethnic identity have also been defined in specific ways. Racial identity has been defined as 'a sense of group or collective identity based on one's perception that he or she shares a common racial heritage with a particular racial group' (Helms 1990, p. 3). Ethnic identity refers to 'one's sense of belonging to an ethnic group and the part of one's thinking, perception, feelings, and behaviour that is due to ethnic group membership' (Phinney and Rosenthal 1992, p. 147). Thus, aspects such as a shared history, common values and beliefs, and customs are important in ethnic group membership, and a sense of belonging to a racial group predominates in racial group identification. Thus, a person may define their racial identity as Asian, but may choose to define their ethnic identity according to ethnicity, for example as Indian, or Punjabi.

It has been argued that race and ethnicity are highly salient for all minority groups throughout their life span (Aries and Moorehead 1989; Thomas, Phillips and Brown 1998). It is important to recognize, however, that the complexities of racial and ethnic identity should not be reduced to race/colour, or cultural simplifications (Gilroy 1987). Robinson (2000) argues that the concept of racialization indicates the social construction of race as a significant dimension in contemporary identities, but that this cannot be an inclusive personal identity. And, other variables, such as gender, age, class, sexual preference and nationality, are important social identities. Other writers have emphasized the fluidity of identity and the notion of a plurality of identities (Hall 1993; Modood, Beishon and Virdee 1994; Reynolds 2006).

Previous research addressing the situation of minority ethnic children and young people in the care system has identified important concerns around racial and ethnic identity (First Key 1987, 1992; Ince 1998). The practice of transracial placement, children and young people being brought up in rural, predominantly white areas, and the lack of positive input around race and ethnicity have been highlighted as key areas of concern. Minority ethnic young people being brought up in their own birth families, in residential homes comprising minority ethnic and white staff, and in multi-racial areas are found to be generally confident and comfortable about their racial and ethnic identity (Tizard and Phoenix 1993; Robinson 2000; Fatimilehin 2002; Barn, Andrew and Mantovani 2005). It is believed that young people in these situations receive good, positive and appropriate racial and ethnic socialization messages from their parents and carers, leading to a good understanding of self and group ethnic identity as well as an awareness of racial oppression and coping strategies to confront racial prejudice (Stevenson 1995).

The pronoun 'we' has been described as encapsulating 'problems in identity, solidarity and difference' (Levitas 1995). It is argued that 'we' can operate as a statement of inclusion (solidarity) on the basis of perceptions of common identity, and simultaneously as a statement of exclusion on the basis of difference. Thus by drawing a boundary as 'we', as a rhetorical statement, and related practices of inclusion, community and communality, it is unavoidable that there will also be a demarcation of 'not we' – of whoever stands 'outside' the boundary that defines who is 'inside' and defined as 'we'. Furthermore, 'sameness' as a criterion for inclusion may repress 'differences' perceived as divisive or contradictory to claims of shared identity. Those who are excluded from 'we' because of perceived differences (as 'not we') experience oppression, marginality and inequality. Given that we know little about the ways in which the process of 'otherization' and the 'we' and 'them' operates for care leavers, it may be useful to explore this in the context of social capital in understanding the negotiation and construction of racial and ethnic identity of young people in this study.

Social capital

Social capital as a concept remains empirically and theoretically contested and elusive. Different theoreticians have sought to operationalize it to provide some guidance on its significance in the lives of individuals and groups. Such writings have ensured the embracing of this concept in public and social policy debates and discussions. Social capital is broadly conceptualized as 'the values that people hold and the resources that they can access, which both result in and are the result of collective and socially negotiated ties and relationships' (Edwards, Franklin and Holland 2003). Some writers have emphasized reciprocity, trust and cooperation (Coleman 1988; Putnam 1995), whilst others have expressed concern about social injustice and inequality (Bourdieu 1991). The work of Coleman and Putnam, whilst important in its ideas of social networks and access to resources, has been criticized for its Eurocentric bias and limited consideration of 'race' and ethnicity (Parekh 2000; Faulkner 2004). Bourdieu's focus on the inter-relationship between social capital and the wider structural divisions and inequality caused by factors such as 'race', class and gender is given greater significance (Reay et al. 2000).

In a paper on young people and social capital, Whiting and Harper (2003, p. 1) define social capital as 'networks together with shared norms, values and understandings that facilitate co-operation within or among groups'. Five key dimensions are identified – social participation, civic participation, reciprocity and trust, social networks and social support, and views of the local area. Given such indicators associated with social capital, which include relationships and networks of trust, reciprocity, mutual obligations and access to families and communities, and conversely absence of resources which can lead to the production and reproduction of inequality, it is worthwhile utilizing the concept of social capital to understand the situation of young people leaving care.

Young people in care, and leaving care, face a range of issues and concerns involving loss and bereavement, geographical uprootedness, loss of family and friendship ties, loss of neighbourhood networks, and instability in care. Minority ethnic care leavers, for whom such factors may be compounded by experiences of racial discrimination and disadvantage, are particularly vulnerable.

This paper seeks to incorporate the work of these different theorists to understand the social networks of care leavers and how these mediate to impact racial/ethnic identity development.

The research study

Aims

Given the weight of previous evidence pointing to poor outcomes for care leavers and the relative dearth of literature concerning minority ethnic young people, one of the key aims of this study was to explore the impact of ethnicity upon social exclusion experienced by care leavers. The study explored the outcomes for young people in a range of areas such as education, housing, employment and training. A particular emphasis was placed on perceived needs and concerns, and support levels. This paper concerns itself only with the ways in which minority ethnic young people sought to make sense of their location in the racial context of British society.

Methodology

The study adopted a mixed-method approach. A range of methods, including a quantitative self-report questionnaire (n = 261), semi-structured interviews, focus groups (n = 36), and an examination of local authority leaving care teams policies and procedures, were employed to elicit information, and to ascertain the views and experiences of young people. The study was carried out in six local authority social services departments in London and central and northern England.

This paper focuses only on the qualitative findings arising from one-to-one interviews and focus group discussions held with young people from six geographical settings in England. A total of thirty-six young people (twenty female, sixteen male) from different and self-defined ethnic groupings participated in the qualitative study. This included young people from a diverse range of ethnic backgrounds, including African-Caribbean (11), African (8), Asian (3), mixed parentage (10), and white (4). A purposive sampling approach was adopted to obtain a good cross-representation of the quantitative sample (which comprised 261 young people) to include adequate numbers of black and minority ethnic young people, and also to maintain a reasonable gender balance.

A semi-structured interview schedule and a topic guide for focus group discussions (FGD) were devised to explore the views and experiences of young people. The major areas explored included preparation for leaving care, experiences since leaving care, housing/homelessness, education/employment/income, health, prejudice/discrimination, relationships and contact with birth family/relatives, foster carers and social workers, and others in the community network, and racial and ethnic identity.

Although this study was successful in obtaining extremely rich qualitative accounts from a number of willing young people, it needs to be recognized that attempting to elicit the views of a vulnerable and highly mobile population can be extremely challenging. It is crucial that the views and experiences of care leavers are documented and taken into account by service agencies in the development of policy, practice and provision.

The study adhered to the ethical principles of the British Sociological Association, and we ensured that our study obtained ethical clearance from the university and from the participating local authorities. Young people were reassured of confidentiality and anonymity, and provided with adequate information to help them formulate informed consent to participate in the study. All respondents were informed of their right to withdraw from the interview or focus group discussion at any stage of the process, and/ or to refuse to answer any questions they deemed to be too sensitive or inappropriate.

Interviews were digitally recorded with the consent of the participants, and were transcribed verbatim. Transcripts were read and re-read to gain familiarity with the accounts of the respondents. This led to an initial coding using key terms related to the research questions. A qualitative software package, Atlas.ti, was used to assist with the computer analysis of the interviews. This procedure enabled a thematic analysis to take place which helped us to manage interview data with greater ease. The possibility of importing data into one easily retrievable place, and being able to generate themes where comparisons could be made and distillation could occur, was significantly helpful.

The following questions are used as a framework to provide coherence and structure to the findings: Do care leavers have access to family and community networks of trust and reciprocity? How does the absence/presence of resources influence care leavers' transition from care and to adulthood? In the absence of key facets associated with 'high' levels of social capital (such as loss of family and community ties/relationships, racial/cultural socialization, lack of appropriate diasporic links), how do young people in care develop individual and ethnic group identities? How are young people themselves engaged in building and utilizing social capital?

The above questions are collapsed into two main areas. Broadly speaking, these focus on the presence and absence of social capital – that is, an exploration of how the presence/absence of social capital can help or hinder the negotiation of a sense of individual and group identity.

Presence of social capital

Research evidence suggests that access to family and community networks signifies levels of social capital (Catan 2004). Arguably, such social capital is vital in the upbringing of children and young people and in inculcating a sense of belonging, trust and reciprocity. Moreover, for minority ethnic children growing up in multi-racial societies it is argued that a process of racial and cultural socialization is in evidence – that is, raising children to be healthy in an environment of extreme stress when perceived negatively by society. Such a process also entails parents' efforts to instil a positive racial and ethnic identity among children, with a particular focus on education and spirituality (Marshall 1995). It is important to conceptualize this process more broadly to explore the ways in which racial and ethnic preparation and messages are transmitted within the wider family and community context.

As discussed above, identity issues are hugely complex for young people separated from their birth families and growing up in care. In a discussion about children from cross-community families in public care in Northern Ireland, Kelly and Sinclair (2005), p. 333) argue that 'promoting a positive self-identity for children requires understanding of a child's family background, including their religion and culture, and consideration of children's group identification, that is, their place in society'. A stable home and community environment are key aspects of such a process.

Research evidence documents that stability and security are essential components for a positive experience in care. We also know that care leavers' lives are marred by instability and placement disruption (Biehal and Wade 1996; Wade 2003; Stein 2006). Our study shows that the majority of young people in this study had spent more than ten years of their life in the care system. Many had experienced severe placement disruption, moving from one foster family to another. In addition to placement instability, young people experienced upheaval in terms of geographical locality and changes in school (see Barn, Andrew and Mantovani 2005). Inevitably, this had a negative impact on young people's relationships, sense of belonging and trust. Given such a volatile context, the extent to which young people were able to maintain a sense of family and community networks, and trust and reciprocity, is questionable.

A number of key factors are said to promote connectedness among care leavers, including education, work, good links with former foster carers, birth family, and other networks in the community (Courtney et al. 2005). Research evidence shows that care leavers have had poor educational experiences and attainment compared to their peers (Jackson and Martin 1998). Contributory factors are said to include poor pre-care experiences, school exclusion, educational and behavioural difficulties, poor communication and co-ordination between education and social care agencies, and inadequate support from carers, teachers and social workers (Berridge and Brodie 1998; Borland et al. 1998; Jackson and Martin 1998). Encouragingly, some recent research evidence shows that looked after young people can achieve educational success given the appropriate support structures, including supportive carers, stability at school and in care, and opportunities to develop hobbies and interests (Jackson and Martin 1998).

In terms of placements within foster families which reflected the young person's own racial and cultural background, Caribbean and white young people were most likely to be placed within such settings. The other groups were dispersed amongst families from a range of different ethnic backgrounds. Moreover, several Caribbean young people reported being placed within a kinship network and the positive influence and stability this provided for them. Conversely, two groups of young people namely white and those of mixed parentage conveyed a history of placement disruption and the instability caused by this.

The notion of trust is crucial in understanding the situation of young people in the care system who experience much instability as a consequence of multiple moves involving substitute carers, high turnover of social work staff, and changes in schooling and geographical locality (Oosterman et al. 2006).

This study shows that most young people of Caribbean, African and Asian background conceptualized their racial and cultural identity to be an important component of themselves. They expressed pride in their cultural heritage, and vocalized the importance of a sense of belonging. Significantly, the majority of these young people were brought up in multi-racial areas; many were placed in families which were racially and/or culturally similar to themselves, and reported receiving appropriate racial/cultural socialization by their carers.

The desire to belong, to fit in, to not be assigned a marginal identity, was in evidence amongst the young people in our study. For Black Caribbean young people, the self-label of 'Black' and 'British' carried an important significance. These young people, whilst recognizing that their parents or grandparents originated from the Caribbean islands, wished to express a strong identification with the label Black British. This was designed to serve the purpose of forging their own unique identity (different from their parents), but also gave them a sense of ownership of the land of their birth – Britain. It signified the contextual and fluid nature of identity (Hall 1993). One young woman echoed the views of many Black British Caribbean care leavers.

I'm Black British, I was born in England ... I'm an English person, I'm British. You don't have to be white to be British.

The complexity of identification with own ethnic group and/or nation was in evidence with regard to Asian and African young people. Both groups expressed a strong identification with their ethnic group culture, and felt that this provided an appropriate individual identity. The significant religious and cultural differences of the Asian group from the dominant white society played an important role in reinforcing difference. In situations where Asian young people reported positive racial and ethnic socialization within the care system, there was evidence of strong individual and group identification. One Asian young man typifies this experience:

> I am Indian ... I love my religion. It has its good points and bad points. At the end of the day I don't want people picking on me, name calling me, because at the end of the day I like it.

Many of the African young people in our sample were born in Africa. They identified with the continent of Africa as their birth place, and expressed a strong attachment.

> I see myself as African, because I was born there ... in school there were lots of races and in debates I was always complaining about colonialism and stuck up for Africa.

Some young people made a connection between cultural mores and values, and place of origin. The different approaches to parenting upheld by people born in the Caribbean, and those of Caribbean heritage but born in Britain, were highlighted. It was also felt that Africans had a more clearly defined value base than people from Europe. Significantly, those who presented as fairly knowledgeable about their cultural background had strong links either with their families or with local members of the community from their country of origin, and emphasized a process by which capital assets are transmitted over time from one generation to the next (Bourdieu 1986). An Asian care leaver voiced the importance of the role of his foster family in transmitting key knowledge and information in the validation of individual and group identity.

> An influence on my culture is having been brought up in this family ... It's very important for me to know my own culture. I'm always asking what's going on now, if they're having a ceremony.

Research literature on social capital identifies young people as consumers rather than producers of social capital (Morrow 2005). In our study, we explored situations in which young people were active in building and utilizing social capital. Moreover, we observed the impact of this in helping to maintain and develop young people's sense of location and belonging.

Racism is regarded as a powerful influence in highlighting difference and marginality and creating divisions. Interestingly, we observed how young people's perceptions of racism also led to a sense of unity. Some minority ethnic young people described having become more aware of their difference in a context where their racial and ethnic difference identified them as 'outsiders', and as the 'other'. One respondent described how her minority status became more 'marginal' when she moved out of London to a predominantly white university in the north of England. The impact of such an experience of marginalization led to group identification whereby this young woman assumed responsibility as an ambassador for her ethnic group.

I think it's because you know I went to a place where there were really no black people. Which was really tough coming from London ... When I'm at University, me and my black friends, we always say we represent black people, because these people don't know what black people are about. They've never been around black people, so whether we like it or not, walking, talking, eating, we are representing the black race.

Absence of social capital

Access to family and community networks is a key indicator of the likelihood of young people's 'embeddedness' and connectedness. Trust and reciprocity are born out of such access to these networks. Our study demonstrates that young people brought up in care are at risk of losing or weakening such ties due to the severe instability they experience during their time in the care system. As highlighted above, transition from care to the community, and from dependence to independence, is an important concern. The section below documents how the absence of resources and networks can influence the process of understanding and negotiating racial and ethnic identity at individual and group level.

Findings from this study show that after leaving care, the majority of the young people had very little or no contact with their birth family. Although there were few ethnic differences between groups, Caribbean young people were more likely to have contact with their birth family than other groups. The frequency of contact, however, did not mean that young people were likely to live with their birth families.

Many of the young people lived alone. African and Caribbean young people were most likely to be living on their own compared with those of white, Asian and mixed-parentage background. Living alone was a difficult and frightening experience for some young people. One

Black British Caribbean young man expressed his fear and apprehension of living alone, and also highlighted the difficult period of transition from care to the community in the absence of family networks and support.

> ... but you know, when you are just not used to actually living by yourself. I'm so used to having been with family or friends or this. So, it was quite difficulty to actually be staying by myself. I still, up to now, find it difficult to be in the house alone. It's only now that I'm actually getting to grips with it ... I get a bit scared in the night, I sleep with the lights on around the house ... I think now I'm getting used to it ... bit by bit ...

The majority of young people lived in areas with a fairly mixed ethnic composition and seemed satisfied with their local amenities. However, very few respondents appeared to have integrated well into their local community, and respondents expressed their uncertainty and lack of skill and knowledge about achieving this. Others were content to keep local people at a distance. From the interviews their sense of loneliness and isolation was palpable as they knew very few individuals in the neighbourhood. For some, the strategy of self-isolation seemed to be a defence mechanism to avoid getting into the 'wrong' crowd. One young woman of mixed-parentage background expressed the typical fear of being drawn into the 'wrong' crowd held by other care leavers.

> I don't know anyone around here at all, and I think that's why I'm staying out of trouble and why I'm sorting myself out. But I don't really want to know no one around here ... and that's not going against them or anything but it's because I don't want to get back into the wrong crowd or whatever.

The absence of role models to nurture and sustain an awareness and appreciation of one's culture was often expressed during the interviews. Many of the respondents told us that they could not identify any major influence in this area, and it was evident that several young people had no real understanding of this concept. By contrast, a young woman of African heritage explained that she had been assimilated into the British way of life to such a degree that she was not sure how she would relate if placed within a community of Eritrean people (her country of origin).

> I've never lived at home, I think culturally I'm 'Britishfied'.

The impact of stereotyping and the inability to nurture children's racial and ethnic identity and to validate this in a positive way was highlighted as a concern by care leavers. A British Caribbean young woman described a lack of understanding within the white care homes in which she had grown up:

> I was living in white care homes ... they stereotypically thought you know just cos I was black I was going to know about West Indian food. You know it didn't matter that ... I could have been an African person, but as far as they were concerned a black person is West Indian. I am, but ... do you know what I mean, it was just stereotypical.

The concept of racial and ethnic identity was clouded by much uncertainty for some mixed-parentage and white young people in our sample. Respondents found it difficult to relate to or discuss meaningfully what constituted a sense of self or what enabled one to develop an identity.

Researchers believe that where 'whiteness' is the norm, white young people are not required to think about their position in society and thus racial and cultural questions of 'where do I belong' are not common. However, some researchers argue that consideration needs to be given to the ways in which white young people conceptualize and locate themselves in a racially ordered society (Nayak 2003).

Minority ethnic young people experience the process of 'ethnicization' where their racial and cultural identity is marked as different in relation to the dominant group (Phoenix 2004). The issue of belonging is said to be of particular importance for those of mixed ethnicity. Researchers and practitioners have concerned themselves with various questions such as: Can they identify with both (in some cases multiple) groups? Do they suffer rejection from both (multiple) groups? Are they at the periphery of each ethnic group, or do they identify with one or both/multiple group(s) (Tizard and Phoenix 1993; Ince 1998; Fatimi-lehin 1999; Aspinal 2009).

In our interviews with white young people, we learned that two of the four white people we interviewed were, in fact, what may be described as of 'mixed-parentage' background, in that their parents came from two different ethnic groups. A mixed-parentage young man of Asian/white background who reported having had no direct or indirect Asian influences in his life described himself as white. It is important to recognize the significance of the notion of 'passing for white'. Thus, the labelling of difference can only take place if the difference is recognized. In this case, this young man recalled no real difficulties in passing off as white.

I feel myself to be White British, but my real Dad was Indian. I haven't seen him for ages, and my mum is British. So it's quite a difficult category to fit into.

A young woman who had described herself as white in the postal questionnaire stated that although she identifies herself as white, her father is in fact a Romany Gypsy. She maintained some contact with her father, and reported that she had learned a few things about the Romany Gypsy culture.

I am white, I'm a white person, do you know what I mean? But I've got that bit of culture in me, and it's not necessarily a race ... well it is a race, but I'm white.

This young woman was herself a mother to a mixed-parentage 4-year-old, but perceived her daughter to be also white. In response to a question about the upbringing of her daughter, and exposure to her racial and cultural background, she believed she lacked the skills and competence to do this as far as the child's Caribbean background was concerned (Harman and Barn 2005).

... It's like it's not down to me to do that, because I don't know nothing about that, so it's down to her Dad ... Because he says she's black, you see, and I'll say she's white cos she looks white.

Most of the mixed-parentage young people in our study were of Caribbean and white parentage, and represented a complex picture reflecting the current debates around mixed ethnicity (Prevatt-Goldstein 1998; Fatimilehin 1999; Alibhai-Brown 2001). Some mixed-parentage young people defined themselves as black, whilst others were vehemently opposed to ethnic categorization, maintaining that this had resulted in a process of labelling individuals without recognizing their right to self-definition.

Confused! Confused would be my identity, I don't know. Every time I see that question I don't know what to put because I'm three different things ... Well I am quarter Jamaican, quarter Spanish, and half English, whatever that makes me ...

It is not surprising that young people who have been separated from their family, and have had limited opportunities to deal with issues of self-identity, should express bewilderment, confusion and anger at society's approach to the ethnic categorization of individuals. What should not be overlooked is how best to achieve reinforcement of young people's identity without imposing a construct that leaves a young person feeling that only part of their heritage is being acknowledged (Barn and Harman 2006).

Many of the mixed-parentage young people in our study had been placed in white or Caribbean families. Almost half of the sample were placed in white families whilst a third were placed in Caribbean families. Those brought up in white families recalled experiences which had been tantamount to 'identity stripping' (Ince 1998).

> I feel that from being brought up in care when I was really young, I lost out ... I didn't really have an identity, cultural or any, I mean one of the places I was put into they changed my name and everything so a lot of my identity was taken away and it was white folk I was living with, so it was like there weren't no positive black role models or nothing. So I did have identity problems if it weren't for going to live with like a few of my family members. I think it was that that brought me closely in touch with my cultural roots, and from then it's like I know who I am now, I like the black side to me. Obviously I'm mixed race so I've got white and black, but I identify with my black roots.

Some young people from a mixed background expressed a sense of clarity and confidence about what they perceived to be their primary identity, that of a black person. This was largely as a result of being defined as such by 'others', or the positive input of relatives and carers (Fatimilehin 2002; Howorth 2002). The significance of these statements cannot be overstated.

> It is important because it's part of your life really ... it's just like even though kids that are mixed race, if a white person was to see me they wouldn't shout 'Oh you half breed' they'd shout 'You fucking nigger' wouldn't they. They wouldn't shout 'Oh whitey, you've got white in you'.

> My Gran is Jamaican and she was the first black person we lived with ... Before I lived with her I didn't think of myself as black, I saw myself as white. But when my Gran told me about my granddad I thought I'm proud of my colour. I am mixed race but I class myself as black.

It was evident that mixed-parentage young people who had been placed with minority ethnic relatives and carers found this to be a positive experience. This was described as an important influence in their construction of the 'Black' identity. It is important to note that these young people had had minimal contact with their white relatives, but they acknowledged their white background.

Conclusion

Although social capital as a concept continues to require ongoing debate and discussion as well as empirical clarity and grounding, our understanding of young people's transitions into adulthood and the multidimensional nature of social capital is growing. However, we still know little about care leavers and their sense of belonging and embeddedness in the community. Moreover, we are lacking in knowledge about how social capital can be utilized to understand the racial and ethnic identity formulations of minority ethnic care leavers.

By drawing upon empirical research, this paper has documented the unstable and precarious upbringing experienced by many young people growing up in care, and the implications of this for young people's transition from care to the community and into adulthood. The effects of placement disruption, geographical upheaval, and absence of stable family and other key individuals in the community have a cumulative impact on care leavers. These factors can result not only in negative outcomes in terms of poor educational attainment, unemployment, homelessness/poor housing, criminal activity, substance misuse, and young parenthood, but may also lead to low self-esteem, low levels of confidence, a lack of belongingness, and feelings of isolation and marginalization.

For minority ethnic young people, separation from family and community can result in poor racial and ethnic socialization. In the absence of key role models and a stable family and community environment, minority ethnic young people may develop a sense of disconnectedness which can lead to questions of belonging and a lack of sense of location in a racialized society. This can hamper the young person's sense of self as well as their ability to deal with situations of racial discrimination.

The accounts of young people in our study demonstrate the complex experiences of growing up in care, and reflect a range of key factors that may be useful in building social capital. It is evident that cultural influences, experiences of prejudice and discrimination, geographical context and ethnicity, and positive racial socialization messages from relatives and carers are important in the development and formation of racial and ethnic identity in young people. Stability and permanence in the lives of looked after young people emerge as crucial considerations for social services children's services. The importance of such family and community stability and its relevance in the building and transmission of social capital to help formulate and strengthen individual and group identity for minority ethnic young people are critical.

References

ALIBHAI-BROWN, YASMIN 2001 *Mixed Feelings: The Complex Lives of Mixed Race Britons*, London: Women's Press

ARIES, ELIZABETH and MOOREHEAD, KIMBERLEY 1989 'The importance of ethnicity in the development of identity of black adolescents', *Psychological Reports*, vol. 65, pp. 75–82

ARMSTRONG, DERRICK 2002 'Pathways into and out of crime: risk resilience and diversity', Economic and Social Research Council

ASPINALL, PETER 2009 '"Mixed race', 'mixed origins' or what? Generic terminology for the multiple racial/ethnic group population', *Anthropology Today*, vol. 25, no. 2, pp. 3–8

BANKS, NICK 1992 'Some considerations of "racial" identification and self-esteem when working with mixed ethnicity children and their mothers as social services clients', *Social Services Research*, vol. 3, pp. 32–41

BARN, RAVINDER 1999 'White mothers, mixed-parentage children, and child welfare', *British Journal of Social Work*, vol. 29 no. 2, pp. 269–284

—— 2001 *Black Youth on the Margins*, York: Joseph Rowntree Foundation

—— 2001 'Racial and ethnic identity', in R. Barn (ed.), *Working with Black Children and Adolescents in Need*, London: BAAF

—— 2006 *Research and Practice Briefings: Children and Families – Improving Services to Meet the Needs of Minority Ethnic Children and Families*, London: DfES, http://www.york.ac.uk/depts/spsw/mrc/documents/QPB13.pdf

BARN, RAVINDER and HARMAN, VICKI 2006 'A contested identity: an exploration of the social and political discourse concerning the identification of young people of inter-racial parentage', *British Journal of Social Work*, vol. 36, pp. 1309–24

BARN, RAVINDER, ANDREW, LINDA and MANTOVANI, NADIA 2005 *Life After Care: A Study of the Experiences of Young People from Different Ethnic Groups*, York: Joseph Rowntree Foundation

BERRIDGE, DAVID and BRODIE, ISABELLE 1998 *Children's Homes Revisited*, London: Jessica Kingsley Publishers

BIEHAL, NINA and WADE, JIM 1996 'Looking back, looking forward: care leavers, families and change', *Children and Youth Services Review*, vol. 18, no. 4/5, pp. 425–45

BORLAND, MOIRA, PEARSON, CHARLOTTE, HILL, MALCOLM, TISDALL, KAY and BLOOMFIELD, IRENE 1998 *Education and Care Away from Home*, Scottish Council for Research in Education, Edinburgh

BOURDIEU, PETER 1986 'The forms of capital', in J.G. Richardson (ed.), *Handbook of Theory and Research for the Sociology of Education*, New York: Greenwood Press

BOURDIEU, PETER 1991 'The peculiar history of scientific reason', *Sociological Forum*, vol. 6, pp. 6–26

BROAD, BOB 1999 'Improving the health of children and young people leaving care', *Adoption and Fostering*, vol. 22, no. 5, pp. 40–8

CATAN, LISA 2004 *Becoming Adult: Changing Youth Transitions in the 21st Century*, Brighton: Trust for the Study of Adolescence

COLEMAN, JOHN 1988 'Social capital in the creation of human capital', *American Journal of Sociology*, vol. 94, Supplement S95–S120

COURTNEY, MARK and HERRING, D.H. 2005 'The transition to adulthood for youth "aging out" of the foster care system', In D.W. Osgood, E.M. Foster, C. Flanagan, and G.R. Ruth (eds), *On Your Own Without a Net: The Transition to Adulthood for Vulnerable Populations*, Chicago: University of Chicago Press

DEPARTMENT FOR CHILDREN, SCHOOLS AND FAMILIES(2007) *National Statistics, First Release*, London: DCSF

EDWARDS, ROSALIND, FRANKLIN, JANE and HOLLAND, JANET 2003 *Families and Social Capital: Exploring the Issues*, Families and Social Capital ESRC Research Group Working Papers Series, no. 1, London South Bank University

FATIMILEHIN, IYABO 1999 'Of Jewel heritage: racial socialisation and racial identity attitudes amongst adolescents of mixed African-Caribbean/White parentage', *Journal of Adolescence*, vol. 22, no. 3, pp. 303–318

—— 2002 'Of jewel heritage: racial socialisation and racial identity attitudes amongst adolescents of mixed Afro-Caribbean/White parentage', *Journal of Adolescence*, vol. 22, pp. 303–18

FAULKNER, DAVID 2004 *Civic Renewal, Diversity and Social Capital in Multi-ethnic Britain*, Runnymede Trust Occasional Paper Series, no. 1, London: Runnymede Trust

FIRST KEY, 1987 *A Study of Young Black People Leaving Care*, London: CRE

—— 1992 *A Survey of Local Authority Provision for Young People Leaving Care*, Leeds: First Key

GILROY, PAUL 1987 *There Ain't No Black in the Union Jack*, London: Hutchinson

GOULBOURNE, HARRY and SOLOMOS, JOHN 2003 'Families, ethnicity and social capital', *Social Policy and Society*, vol. 2, no. 4, pp. 329–38

HALL, STUART 1993 'New ethnicities', in J. Donald and A. Rattansi (eds), *'Race', Culture and Difference*, London: Sage/Open University Press

HARMAN, VICKI and BARN, RAVINDER 2005 'Exploring the discourse concerning white mothers of mixed-parentage children', in T. Okitikpi (ed) *Working with Children of Mixed-Race (Interracial) Relationships*, London: JKP

HELMS, JANET 1990 *Black and White Racial Identity: Theory, Research, and Practice*, Westport, CT: Greenwood Press

HOWORTH, CAROLINE 2002 'Identity in whose eyes? The role of representations in identity construction', *Journal of the Theory of Social Behaviour*, vol. 32, no. 2, pp. 145–62

INCE, LINDA 1998 *Making it Alone: A Study of the Care Experiences of Young Black People*, London: BAAF

JACKSON, SONIA and MARTIN, PEARL 1998 'Surviving the care system: education and resilience', *Journal of Adolescence*, vol 21, no. 5, pp. 569–583

JONES, GILL 1995 *Leaving Home*, Milton Keynes: Open University Press

KELLY, BERNI and SINCLAIR, RUTH 2005 'Understanding and negotiating identity: children from cross-community families in public care in Northern Ireland', *Child and Family Social Work*, vol. 10, no. 4, November 2005, pp. 331–342

LEVITAS, RUTH 1995 'We: problems in identity, solidarity and difference', *History of the Human Sciences*, vol. 8, pp. 89–105

MARSHALL, SHEREE 1995 'Ethnic socialisation of African American children: implications for parenting, identity development, and academic achievement', *Journal of Youth and Adolescence*, vol. 24, no. 4, pp. 377–96

MODOOD, TARIQ, BEISHON, SHARON and VIRDEE, SATNAM 1994 *Changing Ethnic Identities*, London: Policy Studies Institute

MORROW, VIRGINIA 2005 'Conceptualising social capital in relation to the well-being of children and young people', in H. Hendrick (ed.), *Child Welfare and Social Policy*, Bristol: Policy Press

NAYAK, ANOOP 2003 *Race, Place and Globalisation*, Oxford: Berg

OOSTERMAN, MIRIJAM, SCHUENGEL, CARLO, WIM SLOT, N, RUUD, A.R. BULLENS, and DORELEIJERS, THEO 2006 'Disruptions in foster care: a review and meta-analysis', *Children and Youth Services Review*, vol. 29, no. 1, pp. 53–76

PAREKH, BHIKHU 2000 *The Future of Multi-ethnic Britain*, London: Runnymede Trust

PHINNEY, JEAN and ROSENTHAL, DOREEN 1992 'Ethnic identity in adolescence: process, context, and outcome', in G. Adams, T. Gullotta and R. Montemayor (eds), *Adolescent Identity Formation*, London: Sage

PREVATT-GOLDSTEIN, BEVERLEY 1998 'Black, with a white parent, a positive and achievable identity', *British Journal of Social Work*, vol. 29, no. 2, pp. 285–301

PUTNAM, ROBERT 1995 'Bowling alone: America's declining social capital', *Journal of Democracy*, vol. 6, no. 1, pp. 65–78

REAY, DIANE 2000 'A useful extension of Bourdieu's conceptual framework?: emotional capital as a way of understanding mothers' involvement in their children's education', *The Sociological Review*, vol. 48, no. 4, pp. 568–84
REYNOLDS, TRACEY 2006 'Caribbean families, social capital and young people's diasporic identities', *Ethnic and Racial Studies*, vol. 29, no. 6, pp. 1087–103
ROBINSON, LENA 2000 'Racial identity attitudes and self-esteem of black adolescents in residential care: an exploratory study', *British Journal of Social Work*, vol. 30, no. 3, pp. 3–24
STEIN, MIKE 2006 'Research review: Young people leaving care', *Child and Family Social Work*, vol. 11, no. 3, pp. 273–9
STEVENSON, HOWARD 1995 'Relationship of adolescent perceptions of racial socialisation to racial identity', *Journal of Black Psychology*, vol. 21, no. 1, pp. 49–70
THOMAS, KECIA, PHILLIPS, LAYLI and BROWN, STEPHANIE 1998 'Redefining race in the workplace: insights from ethnic identity theory', *Journal of Black Psychology*, vol. 24, no. 1, pp. 76–92
TIZARD, BARBARA and PHOENIX, ANN 1993 *Black, White or Mixed Race*, London: Routledge
WADE, JIM 2003 *Leaving Care*, Quality Protects Research Briefing, no. 6, London: Department of Health
WHITING, ELIZABETH and HARPER, ROSALYN 2003 *Young People and Social Capital*, London: Office for National Statistics

'True stories from bare times on road': Developing empowerment, identity and social capital among urban minority ethnic young people in London, UK

Daniel Briggs

Abstract

This paper is based on evaluative research in an inner-London borough on a programme designed to raise self esteem and deter minority ethnic young people from involvement in crime and participation in gangs. The aim of the programme was to work with young people 'at risk' or involved with gangs, violent crime and who may use weapons and to divert them from this behaviour. Essentially, the paper explores the way in which minority ethnic young people can be equipped to develop social capital. The paper firstly applies a brief contextual understanding of urban minority ethnic young people's experiences of school and 'street life'; secondly, it will describe the background and aims of the programme; and thirdly it will discuss whether and how the programme contributed to developing trust; to notions of awareness and empowerment; self-esteem and identity; and how it impacted on their social and family relationships.

Introduction

This paper is based on ethnographic findings from an evaluation of a charity-funded programme for minority ethnic young people in a disadvantaged area of north London. Data was gathered from observation sessions during the programme and one-to-one interviews with participants once the programme had finished. The programme aimed to work with young people at risk or involved with gangs, violent crime and who may carry/use weapons.

The paper addresses four areas: firstly, it will set the theoretical backdrop for the article; secondly, it will describe the background and aims of the programme; thirdly, it will apply a brief contextual understanding of urban minority ethnic young people's experiences of school and 'street life'; and, finally it will discuss, through the narratives of those who participated, whether and how the programme contributed to developing trust; to notions of awareness and empowerment; self-esteem and identity, and how it impacted on their social and family relationships.

The key question will be whether urban minority ethnic young people can develop social capital to counter the powerful social and structural forces which expose them to 'street life', involvement in crime and gangs. Therefore, for the purpose of this paper, the concept of social capital will be used. Social capital is a useful concept of analysis in this context because it is able to capture the essence of networks, trust exchanges, social support, social relations and social interactions (Putnam 1993). This definition will thus form the theoretical framework for the paper. The paper will begin with a brief examination of social capital, to frame the findings of the study, before discussing the social, cultural and structural conditions of these young people's lives, the methodological approach, and the programme and its impact.

Social capital

The foundations of social capital have traditionally examined dominant classes (Bourdieu 1986; Brown 1994; Franklin 2004; Gatti and Tremblay 2007). Such groups are considered to have 'greater social capital' (Lomas 1998). This is particularly apparent in industrialized countries, where socio-economic inequalities have been found to reduce social cohesion and integration while increasing social isolation (Kawachi and Kennedy 1997; Molyneux 2001): the more socio-economically deprived an area, the poorer access is to 'social capital' (Hefferman 2002). Others, however, indicate that it is entirely relevant for describing social relations among those with limited economic and cultural resources (Stephenson 2001).

While social capital has been linked with increased community cohesion and increased community action for common problem-solving (Narayan and Pritchett 1997), at the same time it is also linked with the increased availability of social capital to offenders (Browning, Feinberg and Dietz 2004). Social capital analyses have traditionally sidelined these groups who may, for example, be involved in or 'at risk of' involvement in crime and anti-social behaviour. It is also evident that social capital has also predominantly explored adults and the communities in which they live; rarely is it used as a tool of analysis for examining young people and youth crime (Helve and Brynner 2007).

However, in her longitudinal Timescape studies, which explored how personal and family relationships develop and change over time, Janet Holland noted how 'poverty, illness, and bereavement, unemployment, drugs, crime, gangs, and violence were endemic on the estate' in a rural deprived community setting. This, she suggested, was 'integral to the young people's lives' in that a 'way out' for young people was largely 'beset with setbacks' and generally considered to be impossible, and even for those who did manage to 'escape the bubble', the pathway was often complex and difficult (Holland 2007, p. 18–19). Those that did manage to increase their career and life prospects relied heavily on notions of social capital. There appears to be little evidence to suggest whether urban minority ethnic young people, when faced with similar structural and social barriers, can prevail by developing social capital.

In addition, it has been argued that the relationship between social capital and ethnicity also remains underdeveloped (Goulbourne and Solomos 2003). Indeed, the same authors have noted how ethnicity is 'a currency of a social capital nature which may be nurtured and invested, squandered, lost, or shared, mixed and utterly changed as a result of meetings at boundary points' (Goulbourne and Solomos 2002, p. 4). Generally, when ethnicity is mentioned, it seems to be in relation to the lack of social capital of inner city ethnic minorities (Putnam 1993).

This is where an examination into minority ethnic young people in deprived urban landscapes becomes important because, broadly speaking, such groups remain at the centre of government, media and community attention; in particular, given that, for a significant number, victimization, street crime and involvement with gangs form some part of their lives at some stage (Briggs, Pitts and Matthews 2007). The term 'gang', however, still appears to be ambiguously understood. It can be a disorganized transient congregation of young people with a common history and biography (Hallsworth and Young 2005), as well as more organized with more criminal and anti-social intent (Pitts 2007). Nevertheless, exposure to influential peers 'on the streets', in some form, involvement in anti-social behaviour and/or crime and difficult family relationships often hinders their life chances and, as a consequence, it becomes difficult to make the most out of education, training, employment and health (Collinson 1996).

Participation in such urban social networks is not always, however, associated with negative results. 'Gangs' or street groups, as Stephenson (2001) notes, can have beneficial consequences. In an analysis of how Russian street children access important resources and networks through social capital, she suggests that children's background plays an important role in their life trajectory in urbanized areas. She found that the street children of Moscow were resourceful and made use of ad-hoc memberships; that: 'they are capable of developing sophisticated social networks which serve their immediate survival needs and can also relate to long-term life plans' (Stephenson 2001, p. 532).

Conversely, and this is perhaps the more hegemonic perspective in the UK, the negative social consequences of these youth networks in urban deprived areas do not always reap such positive results. As Sabates writes, 'one may expect that peers are a protective factor against criminal behaviour but they can also promote anti-social and criminal behaviours' (Sabates 2007, p. 138). This is often manifested in the form of gangs, victimization, anti-social behaviour and youth crime. Gangs, as Portes and Landolt (1996) suggest, are also social networks that provide access to resources and enforce conformity. In the long-term, they conclude, these groups may 'hold people back' rather than 'raising each other up'.

This is set against a structural backdrop of increasing autonomy in the lives of young people, which involves them negotiating a series of complex decisions while simultaneously placing increasing allegiance with their peer social networks. Helve and Bynner note that this increasing autonomy 'supplies the means of resolving identity conflicts and coping with uncertainties on the route to adulthood' (Helve and Bynner 2007, p. 1). Young people are increasingly required to construct their biographies, take responsibility for their lives and make a series of individual decisions, which are often less clear-cut, because they are set within these peer social networks (Raffo and Reeves 2000).

This is important because this not only has implications for how identities are nurtured and how relations are established, but ultimately how the trajectories of young people are shaped. In the context of this paper, this is largely done in the absence of parental supervision and increasingly within the framework of an urban 'street culture'. Therefore, these social and cultural conditions play an important part in shaping their attitudes and expectations, their perceptions of the social world and, more importantly, what it can offer them. Their experiences at home, at school, 'on road' or on 'the streets' in particular play a significant role in shaping their lives and have a more or less direct effect on their motivation to engage in crime and gangs.

Therefore, for the purpose of this paper, such discourses of 'the streets' or 'on road', which have inductively surfaced from this ethnographic research, come to represent the norms, values, conduct and behaviour of young people involved in, or on the fringes of, street crime and gangs. A brief description the programme and its aims will now precede the methodological approach and the findings section of the paper.

The programme and its aims

The aim of the programme was to work with young people 'at risk' or involved with gangs, violent crime and who may use weapons and to divert them from this behaviour.[1] The programme deals with a target group living in a disadvantaged community; this population are predominantly minority ethnic young people. The sessions also aimed to help young people examine themselves, raise awareness of who they are (their identity), improve their family and social relations and explore how society perceives them. The programme involves young people and facilitators sitting in a circle, discussing personal issues. The programme served to complement other youth-orientated programmes in the area by offering a 'hands-on' approach with the local youth population on two deprived estates.

Over eight weeks from June to August 2008, the programme explored young people's issues and helped them identify their goals. Programme sessions took place each Wednesday and Friday from 6pm to 9pm. The programme concluded with a 'residential', which was a four-day excursion in the country. More in-depth sessions were undertaken at this stage. The programme developers, In-volve, commissioned the Families and Social Capital Group at London South Bank University to evaluate the programme. The following section describes the methods used in the evaluation.

Methodology

The research used ethnographic methods including observing sessions and open-ended qualitative interviews.[2] This method was used to gain some practical 'experience' of the programme, observe how young people were affected by the approach of the facilitators, and develop rapport with the young people to enable more fruitful one-to-one interviews at the end of the programme. Over the course of programme, three observation sessions were undertaken with young people and facilitators. Detailed notes were taken and informal conversations were undertaken with young people and facilitators about their experiences. One-to-one interviews were undertaken with fourteen young people who participated in the programme. Interviews were anonymous and confidential. A similar form of ethical commitment was made to observations in the session. Interviews were also undertaken with the facilitators of the programme.

Sample

Overall, thirty-four young people attended the programme, and numbers differed from week to week. They were all from minority ethnic backgrounds and were aged between twelve and twenty-four. Slightly more young women (n = 19) attended the programme than young men (n = 15). The sample of fourteen young people who were interviewed were aged between twelve and twenty-two. Four young people considered themselves to be black African, five black British and five mixed race. Seven of the young people were in school/college and five had some form of employment at the time of interview. Two were unemployed but looking for work.

Validity

Transcripts and field notes were revisited and participants were approached for clarification. This promoted a continual validation of the data, which gradually started to 'sort' out some basic themes which were, at first, descriptive in nature. The final report was shown to three participants for their feedback. Fetterman (1989) has noted that verbatim quotes assist in the process in presenting validity and credibility; this has been also provided throughout. In this opening section, the circumstances of this group of minority ethnic young people in a disadvantaged urban area of north London is contextualized.

Findings

'The streets': a contextual understanding

Evidence from interviews suggests that many urban minority ethnic young people involved in 'the streets' are experiencing what we might call a 'crisis of confidence' and the erosion of their sense of 'self-worth'. Borne, in many cases, of the experience of childhood poverty and troubled family relationships, many have experienced separation and loss and have no consistent father figure in the family home. This is, however, not the whole story, and some of those involved in 'the streets' appear to have experienced none of these disadvantages. Furthermore, to consolidate and often compensate for the absence of parents or extensive family networks, allegiance is pledged to 'the streets', as young people refer to each other as 'fam' (family). This is evident in their day-to-day discourses of growing up and developing peer relationships:

> Hustler: We used to be geeky, like stand outside and play action men and stuff, we were like ten and eleven then we saw all the olders in the ends [older gang members] and they used to beat people up so we thought "let's start doing that" and we started to bully people, kids younger than us, grab hold of them, have a laugh about it and then it got to a point when we started doing it more often and from there it was we were robbing because when I asked my mum for tracksuits, she couldn't do it so I had to keep up and be proper raw [appear 'fresh']. I started robbing loads and beating people up.

Dan: Where was your ends [where did you hang out]?
Hustler: [Place] was where I am from in the blocks. It started to move out to [place] and we met the next lot of boys, start to get to know them and move out and go on days out in other area and used to keep meeting new people "where you from, fam?" "[place] in [place]" and everyone got to know each other.

The experience of school was described by most as 'frustrating' and boring. Indeed, for some time, since the 1990s, it has been shown that young minority ethnic groups were showing evidence of considerable variation in educational achievement (Modood 2004). This has been linked with the fear of 'acting white', which may lead to academically successful black students being disparaged and/or reducing their effort in order to avoid taunts (Cook and Ludwig 1998). Modood (2003) has also indicated that confrontational relationships with teachers, discipline problems and high exclusion rates, plus racial bias in setting (ability grouping) practice as being part explanation for the underachievement of Caribbean male students. Poor facility in English, cultural adaptation, racism and poorly resourced schools have also been associated with the reasons why some minority ethnic groups do less well than national averages (Dwyer et al. 2006). Importantly, however, Modood (2003) states that no one explanation is entirely convincing, but some or all of these issues may account for part of the achievement gap.

Such findings appear to be apparent from this research, and few reflected positively on the experience of school; most became victims of crime and experienced demonization by peers and teachers. Their difficult relationship with school was also associated with a belief that institutional routes to success were unavailable to them. Thus, a culture in which 'avoiding school', 'dropping out' or being excluded appeared to become the option, and 'going solo' and being self sufficient came to be viewed as the only way to retain self-respect and the respect of others. This is a very individualistic world and these beliefs and attitudes can often deter long-term friendships:

When I started reaching secondary school, when I started to see boys get robbed, boys like me, black boys, get robbed. I was like eleven or twelve, bigger boys spitting in other boys faces. It was nice in primary school but it suddenly got worse and then the years after it got worse, people start dying. This is why people are dying – everyone is for their self, they don't care about this and that so I don't trust no one. I trust myself and my mum and my freedom. (Younger Dred)

This individualism notwithstanding, there are immense pressures to conform to the code of 'the streets'. Some authors point out that black Caribbean boys experience considerable pressure by their peers to adopt the norms of an 'urban' or 'street' subculture (Sewell 1997), which is often augmented by the prestige given to unruly and antagonistic behaviour (Strand 2007). This may be, for example, in the use of slang terminology used by young black males which, it has been argued, is socially acceptable and is widely used by white and Asian counterparts. Similarly, it could also be the low hung jeans which derive from the days when prisoners wore their trousers low as belts were forbidden; a look is now considered to be 'cool' among urban youth groups (Okoronkwo 2008).

Meanwhile, these young people tend to be stigmatized for 'hanging around in groups or "gangs"' in the media, and this serves to compound their values and attitudes. For many of these young people, life revolves around creating, establishing and maintaining 'rep' (reputation) among peers and the opposite sex. In this world, money and style are central to the maintenance of 'rep', and young people require material goods to present 'rep', to appear 'fresh' and maintain a lifestyle far beyond what they can actually afford as individuals.

Many cannot or do not rely on money from their parent/s and prefer to 'make it themselves', turning to gangs and street crime not only to sustain their lifestyle but also to increase their rep by demonstrating a willingness to go up against potentially dangerous adversaries:

> Everyone wants to be the biggest, baddest and the most untouchable but if you get robbed people are going to say "you got robbed by so and so" so you are a victim and no one will take you seriously. (Tyson)

This attitude is not limited to boys, for in the narratives of girls it is also evident that the macho world of the streets has implications for the young women who also participate. For them, this means not only adopting the clothes or the language, but also violence:

> More girls are becoming man-dem [like men] ... back in the day I couldn't wait for them to come to my school so we could roll [go on the streets] ... I feel like I'm getting mad old for what these girls are doing. Some boys hate it ... [asking] why is she acting like a man for? (Miss Bruv)
> They're doing what they're doing [the boys] so why can't we too? You join them or you fight them ... you fight it if you act like a brer [boy] ...' (HipChick)

In some urban neighbourhoods, the influence of 'the streets' is there from an early age, but actual involvement in this lifestyle normally presents itself as a choice when young people start secondary school. Some young people flirt with 'the streets', adopting only the style of dress and the language. For them, it is just a 'phase', but nonetheless a phase which can carry many dangers. Others, however, become more heavily involved. Those that do soon grow accustomed to making quick and easy money, contributing to a lifestyle of 'valueless cash', 'easy-come, easy-go'. The more deeply a young person becomes involved in street culture, the greater their financial needs become, because having status on the streets means being seen to have money and being seen to spend it on 'your people' and/or your family. Thus, the deeper their involvement in 'the streets' becomes, the less likely they are to be attracted to the modest rewards from the limited range of legitimate job opportunities available to them:

> £10 cannot last me an hour now, bruv. The way it is, man is getting older, man's needs are becoming more defined and man needs to start earning serious money. (The Prince)

Furthermore, 'the streets' are a powerful influence, but not only upon young people with troubled backgrounds and few prospects. Some participants who were heavily involved in 'the streets' came from stable families and had achieved academic success. One young man indicated how having GCSEs meant very little, as the risk and appeal for the streets was still present: 'It is the area you are brought up in – quite a lot of people go with their environment more than anything else. I know people with GCSEs that are still doing what they are doing [crime] and are influenced about the streets.' Covert Mover, who started out doing street robberies and moved on, via a gang, to more serious forms of crime, has eleven GCSEs, three A levels and had started at university, but also ran a crack-dealing business which yields £1,500 a week:

> It is something that I didn't expect, like once you do something, you get deeper and deeper into things. It is fast cash, easy money, tax free. (Covert Mover)

Moreover, victimization is always a danger, and both male and female participants recognized that, at 'some stage', 'what goes around will come around'. While research has suggested that this is especially apparent in schools in the form of bullying (Smith 2006), it is also apparent in the context of the streets. This attitude was also apparent in the findings as this young girl indicated:

> On the streets anything could happen, anytime so not a new thing – not surprised if people shot or shanked [stabbed]. You can't go

through the street life without being stabbed or beaten. Something will eventually happen to you. (Hipchick)

If, having been victimized, one decides to get 'payback' by fighting one's attackers and/or get back the money or goods or their equivalent, this may well increase one's 'rep' among peers, showing potential adversaries that this not a person who should be challenged lightly. Indeed, Hallsworth and Young (2005)[3] aptly state that:

Men who will retaliate at the slightest provocation. A cycle of retaliation is often inevitable ... 'Feminine' values such as forgiveness, care and compassion are rejected in favour of masculine ideals of strength and power ... Mundane arguments are 're-constructed ... into the stuff of legend.

This can, however, also create a ripple effect, resulting in 'beef' or a vendetta and a sequence of 'comeback' attacks involving ever-larger groups of young people. The notion of 'beef' and potential adversaries is further complicated by the level of suspicion and paranoia about other young people's 'connections'. Although research has confirmed that same ethnic friendship networks are important in identity construction (Reynolds 2007), for a number of young people in these disadvantaged urban environments, such networks, despite having positive values, are often demarcated by postcode boundaries, suspicion of the 'rival other' who may be affiliated with a gang, and general mistrust. These are the often situational and unpredictable day-to-day life contexts that many of these young people face. The next section will examine the programme and its impact across the strands of developing trust, awareness and empowerment, identity and self-esteem, and social and family relationships.

The programme and its impact

The programme sphere: developing trust with adults and peers

The programme took place in a youth club on a deprived urban estate, yet the context and social arena for the programme sessions was respected by all. Facilitators had few problems with young people arriving late or drifting in and out to make or take mobile phone calls. They reflected positively on this freedom to enter and leave the programme as they pleased, and this helped lay the foundations of trust and respect for facilitators. The facilitators were able to 'connect' with young people by using their own experiences as troubled young people also growing up in difficult social conditions. They demonstrated a thorough understanding of the difficulties that minority ethnic young people faced in urban settings and talked openly about their difficult life experiences:

> Marlow [a facilitator], he is your dawg – when he talks, he does make people click and when he tells you about his stuff and it makes you think "a life on streets is not for me". They are genuine people – they are people who did wrong in the past and they are doing good now so Marlow is a good guy, he is talking about how he did wrong in the past and now he works hard for everything which encourages me to put a spring in my step. He is an inspirational. (The Prince)

The facilitators' extensive experience of working with marginalized young people was evident in how they managed the challenging social dynamics of the sessions. One young man, who had been to other youth-orientated programmes, said how it was 'interesting and unique'. He continued:

> In the first session, it was like a general conversation and it was like no one was really talking, but then like Peaches and Marlow started talking about all they had been through and then let us express stuff. They didn't cut us short, like it happens in school because they cut you off, bruv, but there were no boundaries for what you thought or said. (Bravo)

The facilitators were also skilled in assuring confidentiality but also applying support when necessary, since many were not used to releasing information about themselves. This was made more challenging as some young people had 'beef' with each other. Therefore trust had been something difficult for many to employ. Over time, however, a foundation of trust was built within this open forum. This was augmented by 'the residential' which provided a peaceful break from the daily distractions of London life and enabled the expert team 'to deepen the experience' for young people. This was considered to be the most integral part of the programme, as it drew on the eight-week experience which highlighted new levels of trust with peers, but also adults. So much so, new concepts of 'family' appeared in narratives:

> On the residential man, they took us out of the area. There was no TV. The routine is different in the country, nice breakfast lunch and dinner, we did the normal raw sessions, and developed into a family. You can go out there sit on grass, go and see cows and horses, to be real, to do whatever, do your thing, some did that, some went to check the wilderness. (Younger Dred)

The Rock commented that through 'group activities and individual activities', they 'went deep' and 'asked questions which wouldn't be asked so it left us something to think about on a deeper level'. He felt as if he had 'a new family'. Shy H, for example, said that 'everyone was like one big family' and that it was 'like being at home with different people'. She added that had 'we been in the ends [where we hang around on the streets] then none of us would have really knew each other or learn to help each other'. Renegade reflected how it was 'good to learn about each other' and was grateful for the opportunity to go because it kept him 'focused'. The Stacker said he 'bonded with some boys' and, more importantly, found the confidence to 'speak on stage' despite having a 'speech problem'; 'it has really held me back in the past', he concluded.

The euphoria of the event, however, could not last, and most were disappointed to arrive back to London where 'the old life was waiting' (True Stories). 'It was depressing coming back', said Younger Dred; 'when we went off in the coach, we was away from police and dumb people and now you're back it feels like your starting from first'. As relations grew, trust and emotional attachment became stronger, a few admitted they would find it difficult to continue each week without seeing facilitators. For example, The Stacker reflected how he was 'tight with Peaches' and that he would 'miss her'. This prompted some to keep in contact.

Awareness and empowerment

The programme also appeared to promote notions of awareness and empowerment; 'awareness' of current life trajectories and the importance of education and 'empowerment' to feel able to rise above their current social and structural positions to succeed. This was seen as particularly important in how their ethnic disposition was generally perceived – as 'deviant' – which, a few admitted, had often superseded the possibility to 'do other things' or 'lead a better life'. Positive reflections were made about understanding other people's perceptions, perspectives and values. The youngest participant in the sessions described the first moments of her participation: 'we are like in a circle and you talk about stuff that's happened. Like, it is good because you sort of get to understand adults because [adults and young people] they don't understand each other and you learn from doing wrong' (The Queen). For some, to be able to empathize with other people was advantageous:

[The sessions were] good, like it is something to do. Find out things about things and people your never knew, like I don't remember all of it but you interact with people, seeing some of the older and different people there. They are different to on the streets. (Tyson)

Young people were also positive about understanding more about aspects of their daily lifestyle that may have impeded their progress towards life goals. Younger Dred reflected on how he 'learnt new things' about himself; 'how I carry myself, how I am perceived, init. How to be a young man growing up in cruel society and how to get money up legit way' (Younger Dred). An increased awareness of themselves led to them feeling more empowered about their actions. For one young man in particular, who only attended 'four or five sessions', the sessions 'changes your way of thinking' so you 'can understand the consequences of your actions'. He continued by reflecting quite personally on how one session had helped him understand some aspects of his past behaviour:

Basically one of the session was about how you feel, about sleeping around with lots of girls, but if a girl does it they get called names, then thought of perspective of the girls and how they come to their point of view – I respect women more, like me I always used to I think different but that day was a realization. (Bravo)

Discussions were carefully managed by facilitators who carefully helped to point out areas of young people's lives which could be doing more harm than good. In the next field note excerpt, Peaches manages to 'prize open' some of True Stories' dilemmas. While in the circle, she makes a careful dissection of his weed-smoking routines:

7.31pm: A key highlight was listening to True Stories realize how much weed he was smoking when he couldn't afford it (he is on Job Seekers Allowance). He admits that he has stopped smoking weed over the last three weeks because he gets hallucinations and paranoid feelings. This was initiated by Peaches who first of all asks him how much he smokes per day. She then broke it down to how much it costs him per day before summing up how much it costs him per week and per year. In the end, she points out that he smokes £5,000 of weed a year. True Stories cannot believe it and says "I've never thought of it like that." There are a few surprised faces around the room and it is obvious that this resonates with a number of the young people. (8 August 2008)

This learning from each session was linked to the open nature of the discussions, which acted as a channel for young people to talk openly about their life experiences and problems. One young woman was positive that it kept her 'off the streets' and the sessions had become somewhere where 'you can talk about your problems'. She added that 'some people don't know how to talk but it helps you come out of your shell and talk about openly' (Shy H). Even when it appeared that some of the young people appeared to feel restless throughout the sessions, they did not leave the sessions. On several occasions throughout the duration of the sessions, some moments were clearly testing the attention levels of some young people; yet they stayed. Fieldwork notes recorded one such example of The Rock:

> The most poignant moment was watching The Rock, a hardened but shy serious young man, say he could stay only ten minutes but ended up staying forty minutes. He was mesmerized by Peaches' speeches, and he tried hard not to show he was enjoying himself. He was persuaded to play a game which was about being open about feelings. At the end of the game he couldn't necessarily see the fun side of it and reacted like he should punish himself because he didn't win. Later it transpired that he is an artist and poet and has been recovering from the first anniversary of his brother's death. (18 July 2008)

In fact, these moments were aptly summarized in his own words, as he reflected on that first session:

> I loved it [the programme]. I like the fact, when we step into the room, there was a positive vibe, different emotions, a certain level a foundation of trust, not being judged, main key factors. See I came in at the end, two weeks before the residential, just to see what it was all about, and it just continued from there but at first I was cautious. I knew someone who was going to start with and we decided whether we would go in and we went in and they was just expressing themselves and they weren't holding back and it gave me a chance to talk about what is going on in my life and my heart it is always good to make things known if there is a certain agreement about how the information must stay. (The Rock)

In particular, the 'free and open space' which cultivated personal feelings was augmented by the use of the 'truth chair'. The 'chair' was used to 'channel' and disaggregate the emotions and experiences of young people so they could openly connect, understand and share their experiences. With one person sitting in the centre of the group circle, it represented a core feature of the programme which focuses on listening and discussion:

> The truth chair is very good, because it like gives you more confidence, I can't explain it, but to talk openly about yourself

and share personal things with other people but before I wasn't doing this sort of thing. (The Stacker)

Another young man said the programme was useful in that it allowed him to 'release anger' instead of it 'being on the streets'. A few young people, however, found it difficult to sit in the truth chair and talk openly about their feelings and experiences. Shy H, for example, got 'emotional' when it came to 'families and relationships'. Despite feeling more comfortable with people as a result of the programme, she was still reluctant to talk in public: 'I don't know how to talk in front of people, like if I am not comfortable with you, then I can't talk so nothing will come out' (Shy H).

Self-esteem and identity

For me everything was it was good. I think when we had to talk about identity – coz like because it was good, I enjoyed it because talking about identity because you don't think about it and where you go and when you done it and you think who I want to be and how people want to see me, then you feel more confidence about it. (Shy H)

Indeed, before the sessions, Shy H was 'not really focused' on what she wanted to do. 'Really', she said, 'I was with my friends and it was another story'. She summarized powerfully: 'if you don't believe in yourself then you aren't going to get it [what you want from life]'. This is just one of the many examples which reflected the overwhelming increase in a greater sense of identity and enhanced self-confidence among participants. This is suitably summarized by Younger Dred who, aside from attaining a deeper understanding of himself, reflects on how 'the streets' had been a key influencing factor on his 'sense of identity':

I see myself a lot more because even though we are on the road [on the streets] and my trouser hang low, it is the environment that I grew up, and I have to recognize that really I am a king, I am an African king, I am going to be on my way up and be successful and not be a jailcell. (Younger Dred)

Here, however, a realization process has enabled Younger Dred to positively connect with his ethnic disposition and counter negative notions of how his identity had been shaped by his 'environment'. In addition, here negative notions of social capital (being 'on road', involved in gangs and crime) are countered by positive notions of social capital (developing trust and peer relationships) at this seemingly important 'boundary point' (see Goulbourne and Solomos 2002).

In another example, The Rock reflected on how the 'questions of the group' affected him when he was sitting in the 'truth chair'. 'Even when I was hearing what people say when they are sitting on the "chair" it moved me,' he said. He concluded that young people were 'smiling but deep down they are hurting' because they were 'harbouring so much sorrow'. Another young man eloquently said that young people 'walk in masquerading without knowing who they are' but over time, with the help of the 'truth chair', he had noted how 'the image collapses and the mask drops off and you know other people' (The Prince). While this helped young people understand aspects of their identity, the sessions also fostered empathy. This, in turn, helped others step forward to talk about their lives and experiences. Bravo, for example, who thought of himself as someone who was 'stubborn and always right' said he was now more 'dedicated to listening' and 'viewing people differently'. This 'inner understanding' was linked to time spent talking, both collectively and individually, about personal dilemmas.

The deep and discussional nature of the sessions also gave young people the confidence to speak out and express their opinion diplomatically. Bravo, who didn't like 'telling people opinions or views' before the sessions because he was 'cautious of them' said he was able to 'speak out more' and be 'freer' with what he said. Renegade said he was 'all quiet before the sessions'; 'and then you learn how to interact and it made me realize the more open you are the more confident you are'. Increased levels of self-esteem, confidence and greater sense of identity also impacted on behaviour and other aspects of young people's lives. For The Prince, this was helping him to 'curb his anger':

> Like now I am curbing my temper, I do have a short fuse and it only takes one person for me to erupt, something as simple as "hello" can get me going now but now I can control it a bit more. (The Prince)

A few young people did not benefit so much from the sessions, but this was partly linked to the amount of time they dedicated to the sessions. Nevertheless, they still enjoyed the sessions and were positive about its purpose. For example, Tyson, who 'wasn't there much' said it didn't 'do much' for him but that it was 'interesting, something to do and somewhere to go'. The Queen said she had benefited 'a bit' from the sessions, but because she didn't 'go a lot' she didn't 'understand the whole thing'.

Social and family relationships

The sessions, while focusing on elements of young peoples' development of trust, awareness and empowerment, and self-esteem and identity, also drew on elements of their involvement with their family and peer relationships. For this group of young people, the sessions appeared to be more beneficial to their social peer relationships than family relationships. In a few cases, however, family relations were strengthened. Bravo said his family *relations* 'had always been tight' but now they *were* 'tighter'. Younger Dred, who had 'always been a family man', said the sessions had affected him so much that he now sits with his 'family and cousins' and does 'a few small sessions'.

More widely affected by the sessions were peer relationships. This was more closely felt when in the sessions, as a few young people reflected that relations with others attending at the beginning of the programme were negative. Over the course of the programme, however, they had come to respect each other and this had reduced the social pressure between them. In these cases, while they did not become close friends, the sessions helped them accept their opposites or adversaries:

Whatever is spoken, it is between us and the people involved in the programme will experience this power because it does erase certain negative barriers on my part and there was somebody who I knew there [in the sessions], and there was a beef ting [vendetta] with him, but we have to apply things to ourselves too, and now I see him [on the streets] and we are smiling. (The Rock)

There was also acknowledgment that the sessions had impacted on relationships on the street with some young people who attended 'looking out for each other' to 'try to help each other' (Bravo). 'By being together and sharing concern, we get tougher as the day goes by,' reflected The Prince.

Conclusion

This paper has served to build on our understanding of social capital in the context or young people, youth crime (Helve and Brynner 2007) and ethnicity (Goulbourne and Solomos 2003). It began by providing an insight into 'the streets', its associated pressures and risks which urban minority ethnic young people are exposed to, and the kind of tactics which they may employ to 'survive'. Similarly, for many, it summarized difficult experiences with educational institutions, with their families and the increased allegiance to peer networks resulting in increased exposure to 'street life'. Very often, however, involvement in 'the streets' only serves to truncate pathways and limit young people's horizons leaving them increasingly likely to participate in 'gangs' or in street crime. As it has been noted, ways out for deprived young people are often beset with barriers (Holland 2007). In addition, the fact that they are increasingly required to shape their own biography (Raffo and

Reeves 2000) also often leaves them at the mercy of 'street culture' and peer influences. This makes their pathway even more precarious and uncertain and has important implications for their sense of identity.

While it has been suggested that more socio-economically deprived areas have poorer access is to 'social capital' (Hefferman 2002), we can see here that social capital can be developed in such circumstances (also see Stephenson 2001). This programme, though short in duration, has helped minority ethnic young people learn some valuable life lessons at key and pivotal stages in their lives when it is important to lay the foundations for their future, especially set within restrictive social, cultural and structural conditions. As has been evident, however, participating in the programme sessions can help repair trust and build bridging trust relationships (Putnam 1993) between young people and their peers, but also adults.

Similarly, through the sessions, young people have learned about the culture of 'the streets', have learned about their positions of risk and how they have impacted on their lives. They can understand why they participate, how they participate and learn ways to disassociate themselves from these pressures. They are now wiser to potentially damaging daily lifestyles and routines which, for many, involve heavy affiliation to 'the streets' and have 'held them back in the past' (Portes and Landolt 1996). The advantage of this newfound awareness is evident through discourses of empowerment and an understanding of empathy gained through the 'open' nature the sessions. While not all benefit in the same way, it is clear that some participation had some positive result – even for those who rarely attended.

Given that this population are often bereft of opportunity and often influenced by the powerful socio-economic and cultural circumstances of their environment (Briggs, Pitts and Matthews 2007), some foundations for trust, awareness and empowerment were gained through use of the 'truth chair', which helped young people locate deep and troublesome feelings and was managed by skilful facilitators who drew on their experiences of 'the streets', crime and violence. Facilitators helped young people 'look within themselves' – at their inner core – to better understand their identity. They can now have some view into how their identities have been constructed and the powerful forces which have shaped their life trajectories to date. The culmination of this process is achieved in the 'residential', where young people learn about the intimate areas of their identity and further develop strong notions of trust. Group discussions not only help develop trust, empowerment and awareness also strengthen peer and family networks but also help them reassign positive values to negative peer relationships and develop a sense of social cohesion and social capital (Narayan and Pritchett 1997). As Holland (2007) has suggested, developing social capital can benefit disadvantaged young people. This new form of trust and trust exchange has proven to counter previous conflicts between young people, and this transmitted to 'the streets', where these young people had started to 'look out for each other'.

Importantly, where 'ethnicity' has been mentioned it has been in the context of a lack of social capital (Putnam 1993); however, this research has proved that such connections can not only counter powerful social and structural forces but also raise awareness of individual identities and negative constructions of minority ethnic young people. The real test of their newfound trust and improved relations, however, will rest in the crucial period which follows as they attempt to use these new tools in everyday life. While the programme, has helped these young people understand their position and possible new directions in their life, it is difficult to determine what may be the outcome or how they might initiate these newfound 'tools' for their lives. Improved understandings of this area ultimately rest on longer programmes and longitudinal evaluations which continue post-programme. Unfortunately, such funding is rarely considered 'useful' in determining the long-term success of a programme (Matthews et al. 2007) in favour of short term, reactive programmes which will often only go some way to resolving what are often complex social problems.

Acknowledgements

This project would not have been possible without the assistance of the young people who reflected openly and talked freely about their lives, their dilemmas, their experiences and their aspirations. Second, thanks are extended to members of In-Volve for their efficient and organized support: namely Peaches, Sandra White, Marlow Morris and Dinah Senior. Last, but by no means least, thanks are due to Dr Tracey Reynolds, Dr Susie Weller and Professor Janet Holland for assistance with the research.

Notes

1. This did not exclude other groups of young people, who may suffer social exclusion, homelessness, foster care, mental health problems, substance problems, family issues or who come from abused or dysfunctional families.
2. Desk-based research methods using various academic research and use of data collected by facilitators were also used during the eight-week programme.
3. Cited in Firmin, Turner and Gavrielides (2007, p. 28).

References

BAYER, PATRICK, HJALMARSSON, RANDI and POZEN, DAVID 2007 *Building Criminal Capital behind Bars: Peer Effects in Juvenile Corrections*, Cambridge, MA: Florida Department of Juvenile Justice

BOURDIEU, PIERRE 1986 'The forms of capital', in James Richardson (ed.), *Handbook of Theory and Research for the Sociology of Education*, Westport, CT: Greenwood, pp.

BRIGGS, DANIEL, PITTS, JOHN and MATTHEWS, ROGER 2007 *'Robbery Careers': A Research Report Examining Motivations for Robbery, the Victims and Possible Interventions*, London: Lewisham Children and Young People's Directorate

BROWN, GORDON 1994 The politics of potential: A new agenda for Labour, in David Miliband (ed.), *Reinventing the Left*, Cambridge: Polity Press, pp. 113–122

BROWNING, CHRISTOPHER, FEINBERG, SETH and DIETZ, ROBERT 2004 'The paradox of social organisation: networks, collective efficacy and violent crime in urban neighbourhoods', *Social Forces*, vol. 83, no. 2. Pp. 503–34

COLLINSON, MIKE 1996 'In search of the high life: drugs, crime, masculinity, and consumption', *British Journal of Criminology*, vol. 36. no. 3. Pp. 428–44

FETTERMAN, DAVID 1989 *Ethnography: Step by Step*, London: Sage

DWYER, CLAIRE, MODOOD, TARIQ, SANGHERA, GURCHATHEN, SHAH, BINDI and THAPER-BJORKERT, SURUCHI 2006 'Ethnicity as social capital? Explaining the differential educational achievements of young British Pakistani men and women', Paper presented at the 'Ethnicity, Mobility and Society' Leverhulme Programme Conference, University of Bristol, 16–17 March

FIRMIN, CARLENE, TURNER, RICHARD and GAVRIELIDES, THEO 2007 *Empowering Young People through Human Rights Values: Fighting the Knife Culture*, London: Esmee Fairburn Foundation

FRANKLIN, JANE 2004 *Politics, Trust and Networks: Social Capital in Critical Perspective*, London: London South Bank University

GATTI, UBERTO and TREMBLAY, RICHARD 2007 'Social capital and aggressive behaviour', *European Journal of Criminal Policy Research*, vol. 13, pp. 235–49

GOULBOURNE, HARRY and SOLOMOS, JOHN 2002 *Ethnicity Strand Working Outline*, unpublished document, Families and Social Capital ESRC Research Group, London South Bank University

GOULBOURNE, HARRY and SOLOMOS, JOHN 2003 'Families, ethnicity and social capital', *Social Policy and Society*, vol. 2, no. 4, pp. 329–38

HALLSWORTH, SIMON 2005 *Street Crime*, Cullompton, UK: Willan Publishing

HALLSWORTH, SIMON and YOUNG, TARA 2005 'Getting Real About Gangs', *Criminal Justice Matters*, vol. 55, pp. 12–13

HEFFERMAN, CHIASSON 2002 'HIV, sexually transmitted infections and social inequalities: when the transmission is more social than sexual', *International Journal of Sociology and Social Policy*, vol. 22, pp 159–76

HELVE, HELENA and BYNNER, JOHN 2007 'Youth and social capital' in Helena Helve and John Bynner (eds), *Youth and Social Capital*, London: The Tufnell Press, pp.

HOLLAND, JANET 2007 'Inventing adulthoods: making the most of what you have', in Helena Helve and John Bynner (eds), *Youth and Social Capital,* London: The Tufnell Press

MATTHEWS, ROGER, EASTON, HELEN, BRIGGS, DANIEL and PEASE, KEN 2007 *Assessment of the Outcomes of Anti-Social Behaviour Orders*, Bristol, UK: Policy Press

MODOOD, TARIQ 2003 'Ethnic differentials in educational performance', in David Mason (ed.), *Explaining Ethnic Differences*, Bristol, UK: Policy Press

MODOOD, TARIQ 2004 'Capitals, ethnic identity and educational qualifications', *Cultural Trends*, vol. 13, no. 2, pp. 87–105

NARAYAN, DEEPA and PRITCHETT, LANT 1997 'Cents and sociability: household income and social capital in rural Tanzania', World Bank Research Paper No. 1796, Washington, DC: The World Bank

OKORONKWO, NDUBUISI 2008 'The phenomena of black youth crime and how black youths are portrayed in the media in the United Kingdom: whether the portrayal can be considered exaggerated, or if the moral panic is in someway justified?' Internet Journal of Criminology, http://www.internetjournalofcriminology.com/Ndubuisi%20-%20Phenomena%20of%20Black%20Youth%20Crime%20and%20Media%20Reporting.pdf

PORTES ALEJANDRO and LANDOLT, PATRICIA 1996 'The downside of social capital', *The American Prospect*, vol. 26, May–June, pp. 18–21

PUTNAM, ROBERT 1993 'The prosperous community: social capital and community life', *American Prospect*, vol. 4. no. 13, pp. 35–42

RAFFO, CARLO and REEVES, MICHELLE 2000 'Youth transitions and social exclusion: developments in social capital theory', *Journal of Youth Studies*, vol. 3. no.2, pp. 147–66

SABATES, RICARDO 2007 'Education and juvenile crime: understanding the links and measuring the effects', in Helena Helve and John Bynner (eds), *Youth and Social Capital,* London: The Tufnell Press

SEWELL, TONY 1997 *Black Masculinity and Schooling: How Black Boys Survive Modern Schooling*, Stoke-on-Trent, UK: Trentham Books

SMITH, DAVID 2006 *School Experience and Delinquency at Ages 13 to 16*, Edinburgh: The University of Edinburgh, Centre for Law and Society

STEPHENSON, SVETLANA 2001 'Street children in Moscow: using and creating social capital', *The Sociological Review*, vol. 49, no. 4, pp. 530–47

STRAND, STEVE 2007 *Minority Ethnic Pupils in the Longitudinal Study of Young People in England*, Nottinghm, UK: DfES Publications

Young people's social capital: complex identities, dynamic networks

Susie Weller

Abstract
Social capital has become an increasingly popular concept in policy
discussions surrounding integration and social cohesion. Within the UK,
numerous policy-makers have drawn heavily on the work of influential
social capital theorist Robert Putnam, whose recent thinking has been
implicated in debates concerning identity, diversity and cohesion. What is
meant by 'diversity' is subject to conjecture. Arguably, identities and
affiliations are more complex than often presented in social capital
debates. Drawing on material from an ongoing longitudinal study, the
paper addresses the relative neglect afforded to young people's networks
and resources by focusing on the role many play in creating social capital
within families. Acknowledging the significance of time and space, the
paper explores the interface between different aspects of identity and
the dynamic nature of social networks. In doing so, the need to take a
more nuanced and context-sensitive approach to the analysis of social
capital is highlighted.

Introduction

Social cohesion and the fostering of inclusive neighbourhoods that
value 'diversity' increasingly feature as a central component of UK
Government policy (Dwyer et al. 2006; Hetherington et al. 2007;
Dunnell 2008; Dwyer and Bressey 2008). Indeed, in 2007, a legal
obligation was placed on schools to promote such cohesion (DCSF
2008). In recent years, social capital has become an increasingly
popular concept in policy debates surrounding social exclusion and
cohesion on both sides of the Atlantic (Schuller, Baron and Field 2000;
Field 2003; Franklin 2004). Numerous policy-makers have drawn

heavily on the work of influential social capital theorist Robert Putnam (2000, 2007), whose recent thinking has been implicated in debates surrounding identity, 'Britishness' and the notion that, in the short-term, increasing diversity has a detrimental affect on neighbourhood solidarity (Putnam 2007). Somewhat problematically, there has been a tendency to equate diversity with particular categories of identity, namely ethnicity, religion and, to some extent, class. What is meant by 'diversity' is, however, subject to conjecture. Arguably, identities and affiliations are more complex than often presented in social capital debates. Rob Berkeley (2002) argues that as a precursor to policy formulation many questions surrounding the nature of diversity need to be resolved. In seeking to shed light on such issues, this paper focuses on young people's experiences; a 'group' whose perspectives have, until late, been afforded little attention within social capital debates. In doing so, I seek to contribute conceptually to the growing body of work that focuses on the role many young people play in initiating and creating social capital within families, schools and neighbourhoods, as well as, providing insights of relevance to policy-makers and practitioners (see, for example, Morrow [1999]; Bassani [2003]; Schaefer-McDaniel [2004]; Helve and Bynner [2007]; Holland, Reynolds and Weller [2007]; Weller [2007a]; Holland [2008]).

Drawing on material from an ongoing Qualitative Longitudinal study, this paper explores the interface between different aspects of young people's identities, the nature of their social networks and the role many play in initiating different forms of social capital within families (for a focus on 'schools' or 'neighbourhoods' see Weller [2009]; Weller and Bruegel [2009]). In doing so, the need to take a nuanced and context-sensitive approach to the analysis of social capital is highlighted.

Social capital, young people and identity

Despite a burgeoning literature, what constitutes social capital remains relatively ambiguous, with influential authors such as James Coleman, Robert Putnam and Pierre Bourdieu providing alternative under-standings and applications of the concept (Schaefer-McDaniel 2004; McGonigal et al. 2007; Holland 2008). Coleman, Hoffer and Kilgore (1982) employ social capital to explore differences in educational outcomes, whilst Putnam's (1993, 2000) focus is on civic engagement. Both share common ground, viewing social capital as a positive entity; a means of fostering trust, cooperation and integration (Coleman 1990). Alternatively, Bourdieu (1986) examined the reproduction of class advantage, regarding social capital as part of a bundle of different forms of capital, important for social injustice and equality (Field 2003; Holland, Reynolds and Weller 2007). Despite its elusive definition, there are commonalities uniting a range of authors, not least a focus on norms, trust, values and networks (Granovetter 1973; Putnam 2000; McGonigal et al. 2007). This paper is framed by a broad understanding that defines social capital as the resources individuals and collectives derive from their social networks. Social capital is not an 'object' but rather a set of interactions and relationships based on trust and reciprocity that have the potential to be transformative (Weller 2006).

'Youth' is commonly regarded as a significant stage in the life-course in terms of identity development (Kuusisto 2007). In discussing young people's social capital, authors such as Helena Helve (2007) and Tracey Reynolds (2007) have highlighted the significance of social networks in identity formation. Furthermore, James Côté (2007) talks of 'identity capital', suggesting that 'social capital networks activate relational aspects of identity' (2007, p. 62). Young people's multi-farious identities are, therefore, implicated in the nature of their social networks and the resources which they acquire from those connections. In turn, different forms of social capital can enable the creation of new identities or the (re)affirmation of particular aspects of self. Whilst this paper seeks to highlight the complexity and overlapping nature of young people's identities, particular emphasis is placed upon ethnic identity and cultural affiliations. Such a focus not only corresponds with the broader themes of this special issue, but also seeks to bring a more nuanced perspective to social capital debates where ethnic identity is often something imposed from the 'outside' (Goulbourne and Solomos 2003).

Central to exploring the connections between social capital and identity rest questions about the nature and strength of ties. In recognizing different forms of social capital, Putnam (2000; 2007) adopts a two-fold typology comprising *bonding* and *bridging* elements, whereby the former refers to exclusive, inward-looking connections amongst homogenous groups, whilst the latter denotes outward-looking networks between different groups (for other forms, see Woolcock [2001]). Whilst to some extent such distinctions can prove fruitful for exploring the nature of social networks, it is important to reflect critically on the categories and boundaries used to demarcate 'difference'. For Putnam (2007), 'diversity' is primarily defined in terms of ethnicity, race and to some extent economics. Taking a quantitative stance, his work utilizes, somewhat uncritically, 'catch-all' US census categories for ethnicity, namely Hispanic, non-Hispanic white, non-Hispanic black, and Asian. Despite alluding to the fluidity of diversity, Putnam pays sparse attention to the ways in which individuals conceive of their own (ethnic) identities and those of others. Alternatively, several authors have focused on social capital and different aspects of identity, including friendship, the attainment of different ethnic groups and transnational networks of care (Zhou 2005; Dwyer et al. 2006; Reynolds and Zontini 2006; Reynolds 2007). Drawing on young people's accounts, this paper is concerned with the neglect afforded to the complexity and multiplicity of identity within dominant social capital debates.

Whilst social capital features heavily in a number of policy agendas, influential theorists have tended to view young people as passive in the formation of social capital within families and communities (in all their multifarious guises). For example, Coleman (1990) talked of children as future beneficiaries of their parents' social capital through the advantages of academic achievement. Similarly, Putnam's (2000) focus centres on the importance of parental social capital on a child's development. Whilst Bourdieu's (1986) notion of social capital does include children, it is still principally centred on their future rather than present lives. In these terms, social capital is essentially posited as a one-way process placing little value on young people's agency. More recently there has been growing interest to the contrary, with a number of authors concentrating on young people's *own* social capital in a variety of contexts, including community involvement, education and health (Morrow 1999; Bassani 2003; Schaefer-McDaniel 2004; Helve and Bynner 2007; Holland, Reynolds Weller 2007; Weller 2007a; Holland 2008). In this study, many participants drew upon their social networks to access a range of cognitive, emotional and social resources (Weller 2007a). Moreover, and, as this paper demonstrates, many were instrumental in creating and shaping the networks of others.

Considerations of social capital also warrant a context-sensitive analysis. Indeed, both *time* and *space* are influential in shaping the nature of networks and identities. Although authors such as Putnam have focused to some extent on time, concern has primarily been centred either on linear understandings or on the relationship between time-use and social capital development (for a detailed review, see Gray [2003]). A temporal perspective not only highlights the dynamic and evolving nature of social capital (Goulbourne and Solomos 2003; Weller 2007b) but allows for the consideration of young people's networks in the here-and-now. Similarly, a spatial perspective illuminates the ways in which different arenas bring to the fore particular aspects of identity and, in doing so, shapes opportunities for developing different connections and networks. For many young people in our study, time spent within different spaces – for example, schools, colleges, places of worship, leisure activities, public and commercial domains – provided different opportunities for forging 'bonding' and/ or 'bridging' social capital.

Researching young people's social capital over time

This paper presents findings from an ongoing Qualitative Long-itudinal study[1] that broadly seeks to chart change and continuity in young people's lives. Based in the UK, the research forms part of *Timescapes*,[2] an Economic and Social Research Council [ESRC] programme that documents relationships and identities across the life-course. Our study tracks the lives of fifty-two young people who participated in one of three studies conducted by the Families and Social Capital Research Group between 2002 and 2005. As such, this original material constitutes Wave One of our current longitudinal work. Wave Two was completed in 2007, whilst Wave Three is currently underway. Here I draw upon material from waves one and two.

Importantly, this paper focuses on the accounts of three young people drawn from *one* of the original studies;[3] a four-year project that explored children's experiences of secondary school transfer (Weller 2007a; 2007b; 2009). A focus on social capital and the diversity of children's networks formed an explicit part of our work, and emphasis was placed on the ways children utilized their social capital to enable them to settle into their new school. The research was conducted in two phases (pre- and post-transfer), and used a mixed-method approach to document the experiences of children from a diverse range of backgrounds and living in five different locations marked by intense competition for school places. During the pre-transfer phase, 588 eleven year-olds in their final year of primary school (twelve schools) took part in Survey 1, which explored changes respondents anticipated during secondary school transfer. At the time, seventy-six parents, recruited via the case study primary schools, took part in an interview, which explored the deployment of social and economic capital in the school admissions process. During the post-transfer phase, eighty-one respondents completed Survey 2, which also asked them to reflect upon change and continuity. Focus groups with seventy-five young people were then used to determine peer group perspectives across a range of school types. Finally, in order to glean more nuanced accounts of personal experiences, individual interviews were conducted with twenty young people.

Our follow-up work entails a slightly different focus, with social capital and the diversity of young people's social networks forming a more implicit element. Rather, Wave Two is concerned with charting the meanings, experiences and flows of young people's chosen (friendships) and prescribed (sibling) relationships. We also aim to explore how such relationships relate to young people's sense of self as their individual and family biographies unfold. Participants from all three original studies were invited to take part in two waves of follow-up work. The resultant sample of fifty-two young people is nationally distributed across England, Scotland and Wales. Data have primarily been gathered via in-depth semi-structured interviews conducted either with individual young people or small sibling groups, dependent on participants' preferences. Akin to Wave One, we have used a range of methods, including in-depth interviews and children-centred activities such as network maps, timelines, diaries, vignettes and photography.

In both waves, the ethical and methodological issues involved in research with children and young people have been afforded significant attention. Issues such as informed consent, confidentiality and anonymity and power have been particularly pertinent in such contexts (Barker and Weller 2003). Whilst the studies may not be deemed fully participatory, we have sought to involve young people in the research process via our panel of young advisors. Participants chose their pseudonyms, which are used throughout the paper.

Responding to Rosalyn George's (2007) assertion that the friendship networks of minority ethnic young people have been overlooked, this paper focuses on the lives of three young people:

Jay lives with her parents and brother in a terrace house in East London. Whilst Jay was born in the UK, she has strong family connections with a region of Southern India. Jay is a practising Hindu and attends an all-girls school. Her father works for a manufacturing company and her mother works with children part-time.

Michael lives with his parents and two brothers in a small terrace house in South London. Michael's parents moved to London from Nigeria and he was born in the UK. Michael attends a selective Catholic boys' school and both his parents work in public services.

Kiera lives with her parents and sister in a small flat in East London. She was born in Hong Kong to Vietnamese parents. Her family migrated to the UK a decade ago. She attends a Catholic girls' school and a Vietnamese Catholic church. Her father works as a printer and her mother is a full-time home-maker.

The examples presented are not intended to be representative but rather are illustrative of the need to take a nuanced approach to the analysis of social capital.

Actively *creating* social capital within families

Until recently, young people have been posited as passive within many social capital debates. Our work, however, suggests that the formation of social capital within families can be viewed as an interactive process, with different family members and friends each shaping the networks of, and providing resources for, others. Parents may influence the nature of their child's social networks by seeking out schools or activities characterized by differing degrees of class-based, ethnic, gender and/or religious diversity/homogeneity (Smith and Khanom 2005; George 2007). In turn, young people can, both directly and indirectly, influence the networks of their parents and siblings (McGonigal et al. 2007; Weller and Bruegel 2009).

Education policies, particularly those promoting parental choice and the diversification of school types, also shape the social networks of different family members (Weller 2009). Access to different schools is by no means equal, with class, ethnicity, faith, gender and social capital bound up in the opportunities available to different young people (Reay and Ball 1998; Ball 2003). Michael's story provides a pertinent example. Michael's parents migrated to the UK from Nigeria and, in seeking a better quality of life, were ambitious for their sons. Despite limited economic capital, Michael's mother, Folami, was able to negotiate access to a highly sought-after Catholic school by drawing on the social capital she developed through their local Catholic church. In selecting such a school, Folami sought to shape the networks of her sons, encouraging friendships that 'bridged' across class and ethnic boundaries but were 'bonded' by faith and situated within a particular value system (Kuusisto 2007). Salient to Michael's social capital was his mother's drive to instil values such as discipline, respect and strong family bonds, which she regarded as emanating from her own cultural heritage and framed by faith-based values and norms. As a result, Michael demonstrated a real sense of connectedness and willingness to support his siblings:

> I think you should help your brother with their work because sometimes if I get stuck I ask my older brother and he'll help me so it is good 'cos what *you* know could always help if you pass it on to your little brother.

For Michael's parents, the support exchanged by the brothers proved invaluable in reaffirming their own values and in enabling them to engage more fully with an education system with which they felt unfamiliar. The school also instigated opportunities for parents to meet and, in turn, the brothers knew each others' friends. Such examples illustrate the means by which the networks of different family members are often inter-connected.

Likewise, Kiera's networks outside school were interrelated with those of her family. Since migrating to the UK, Kiera and her family have established strong links with the local Vietnamese community. She regularly attended a Vietnamese Catholic church and local cultural groups/activities, including dance classes and Vietnamese lessons. As such, these associations formed the backbone of her social life and signified the main arenas through which the family developed local social capital. Kiera's parents, for example, drew on their own 'bonding' social capital to help their daughter with her schoolwork. Kiera described one such relationship:

> she's older than me ... her parents and my parents know each other ... I usually go around the house and play sometimes and go eating in restaurants and yeah, she helps me with my homework ...

At the same time, Kiera also shaped the networks of her immediate family. She sometimes acted as translator for her mother, who spoke little English, potentially enabling the development of 'bridging' social capital. Her sister also considered the younger siblings of Kiera's friends as her own companions. Such interconnectedness highlights how the networks of different family members can be mutually reinforcing of trusting relationships. At the same time, closely 'bonded' networks can prove limiting. Over time school friends, from a range of backgrounds, became more significant to Kiera, but her mother continued to encourage friendships with those of a similar (Vietnamese-Catholic) upbringing. Indeed, school represented the only arena in which Kiera could establish social capital independent from her family.

Whilst Jay has spent all her life in East London, 'back home' for her referred specifically to the Indian State in which her mother was born. Encouraged strongly by their father, Jay and her brother primarily spoke in their mother's regional dialect whilst at home and attended tuition classes[4] organized by the allied community association. Her mother's identity and heritage played an important role in shaping Jay's own sense of self. Connections within the community association afforded access to a wide range of resources, and many of Jay's friendships were interconnected with those of her family:

> this is my dad's cousin but we're really, really close and I can say anything to her literally ...

During Wave One, Jay had school friends from a range of ethnic and faith backgrounds, although her tuition class friends, people she associated with outside school, were cited as her closest relationships. She experienced difficulties at school and turned to her tuition class friends for support. Jay appeared to view the 'bonding' social capital she developed via inter-connections with her parents' networks as empowering, enabling her to develop confidence, resilience and a strong sense of self. Over time, although Jay's identity remained shaped by an enduring connection to her mother's heritage, she began to forge stronger ties at school with girls from different backgrounds. Viewing such bonds as family-like, her new relationships provided a range of resources, not least support and guidance. Concurrently, her tuition class friends became less significant; a change partly accounted for by fears over surveillance and her brother's inter-connectedness with these friendships. Jay's investment in specific aspects of her identity and her connections with others who shared similar cultural, ethnic and faith backgrounds helped foster a strong and resilient sense of self, which over time enabled her to 'bridge out' to different networks and develop social capital independent from her family.

The examples cited highlight the need to view the formation of social capital within families as an interactive process. Nonetheless, it is also important to consider the complexity of young people's identities and networks.

Looking *within* and *beyond* broad categories of identity

The findings that follow demonstrate the fundamental need to look both *beyond* and *within* broad categorizations of identity in order to render social capital debates meaningful (George 2007). Such classifications often focus on visible features, thus failing to reflect individual's understandings of their own identity and sense of belonging to, or affiliation with, different groups. Indeed, much can be gleaned from Alastair Bonnett and Bruce Carrington's (2000) critique of the essentialism inherent in imposing such categories (see also Dwyer and Bressey [2008]). As part of our survey work, participants were invited to describe similarities and differences between themselves and their friends. Shared interests and personality (including attitude towards school) were common responses, with few referring explicitly to either religion or ethnicity (Weller 2009). Many participants also shed light on the challenges inherent in defining different aspects of identity. In Survey 2, participants were invited to describe openly the ethnic backgrounds of their friends. A number of participants were keen to highlight 'mixedness' or 'hyphenated identities' (Bonnett and Carrington 2000; Caballero, Edwards and Puthussery 2008). For example, when detailing her best friend's ethnicity, one participant wrote, 'black, white African-Jamaican', whilst another respondent described herself as 'African black but born in Italy'.

Jay serves as a prime illustration of the importance of looking *within* 'catch-all' ethnic categories. In describing her ethnicity in Survey 1, Jay selected 'Indian' from a range of options. She also chose to write about the languages she spoke, including a regional dialect from the Indian State in which her mother was born. When detailing her friendships, 'being Indian' featured as an aspect of her identity she shared with some of her friends, whilst language and, in one instance, religion were documented as differences. Around eighteen months later, Jay completed Survey 2. Rather than refer explicitly to 'being Indian' as a shared point of connection amongst her closest friends, Jay cited their (out-of-school) tuition class as a commonality; an implicit reference to her involvement with the aforementioned community association. The specificity of Jay's identity as not just 'Indian' transpired as fundamental in the development of her own social capital. Again, pointing to a more nuanced understanding of difference, Jay alluded to the intricacy of ethnicity when describing her friendships at secondary school:

> she's Mauritian, she's Sri Lankan, she's Tamil ... Tamil ... Malayalee ... Nigerian ... so and the rest are Gujarati all mixed together!

Following Claire Dwyer and Caroline Bressey's (2008) notion of *lived ethnic identities*, the intersections between different aspects of identity are significant, for they may shape the nature of young people's networks. In our study, Kiera's narrative was imbued with gendered notions of friendship, and she made many references to the importance of 'talk' and 'trust' as friendship-based resources (Lawhon 1997). Throughout our research, Kiera had two quite distinct sets of social networks. Firstly, she attended a Catholic girls' school, and whilst her relationships were generally 'bonded' by faith and gender, she described her networks as ethnically diverse, comprising girls from African and Caribbean backgrounds. Using conventional categories of 'difference', these connections may be described as simultaneously 'bonding' and 'bridging'. Secondly, outside school Kiera's networks appeared very different, comprising friendships established through her family's connections with the local Vietnamese community and associated Catholic church. These were long-term relationships that provided a wide range of resources, including inspiration, guidance and support. United originally by their Vietnamese-Catholic connections, Kiera and her closest friends have since developed a number of common interests, which are now equally important in 'bridging' their relationships as family background:

> four Vietnamese friends of mine ... yeah ... we all have things in common like TV programmes, music, fashion ...

Arguably, notions of identity need to be fluid, as individuals and groups often identify with different aspects simultaneously (Mand and Weller 2007). In these terms, the distinction between what constitutes 'bonding' and what represents 'bridging' social capital becomes less clear-cut. A connection that constitutes 'bridging' in one context may represent 'bonding' in another (Weller 2009).

Whilst it was beyond the realms of the study to engage fully with young people's religious identities, it was apparent that religious values and norms framed the ways in which some parents raised their children and also shaped young people's identity formation and acquisition of social capital (see Kuusisto 2007). Building on findings from Greg Smith and Afsia Khanom's (2005) study, which explored children's understandings of the role religion plays in shaping their identities and networks, Michael's example highlights important intersections between religion, culture (including parental upbringing), ethnicity, gender and social mobility. During Wave One, Michael defined himself as both 'black British' and 'West African' and, whilst born in the UK, he alluded to his parents' country of birth as part of his own identity:

I tried to understand a native language from *where I'm from* but it's quite hard ...

Echoing Claire Dwyer et al.'s (2006) assertion that those from middle-class backgrounds are more likely to exhibit 'bridging' social capital, Michael valued 'difference', believing it fundamental in uniting friends:

The first two [friends] are ... very English and then the other two ... one is from South America and one is from Sri Lanka so from different cultures but that's sort of why we can talk to each other ... different cultures so we are learning from each other.

Whilst Michael's family would not conventionally be classified as middle-class, the nature of his school and social life meant that much of his time was spent in all-male, faith-oriented, middle-class contexts. Even though he recognized cultural and ethnic differences, common-alities principally based on gender, religion and class/mobility remained 'unspoken'. Importantly, intersections between different aspects of identity are not always explicit in participants' narratives. There is, therefore, an underlying ambiguity inherent in isolating which aspects of identity *matter* in shaping networks in different contexts.

As the examples imply, it is important to regard identities as layered and subjective and to explore underlying intricacies and multiplicities. The adoption of 'catch-all' categories is likely to present a partial or even distorted picture of young people's networks (Weller 2009).

The significance of *time* and *space*

A context-sensitive approach focusing on time and space is arguably central to providing a nuanced account of 'diversity' in young people's networks. The spaces young people occupy at different times provide a range of opportunities to initiate and create different types of social capital. Schools, for example, are fundamentally influential in fostering social connections, and, therefore, are implicated in shaping identities. Moving to secondary school, for instance, enabled some young people to develop connections that they felt allowed the (re)affirmation of specific aspects of their identities, whilst others sought and valued connections across (perceived) dimensions of difference (Smith and Khanom 2005; George 2007, Weller 2009). As the previous sections have demonstrated, Jay's connections and relationships with a local community association have shaped fundamentally the nature of her networks. For Jay, her school, temple, community association and tuition classes provided the primary sites in which she fostered social capital. One pertinent example of the significance of space was her ambivalent connection to the Indian state she referred to as 'back home'. Whilst the family visits the region every few years, connections to family members 'back home' were relatively intermittent. Nonetheless, Jay's networks in the UK and her involvement with the community association formed the backbone of her ethnic/cultural identity. In India, other aspects of her identity were salient:

> we [Jay and her brother] both moan a lot ... insects ... no English things ... we still miss our English touch when we go back home, especially for 4–6 weeks ... 'Oh my God, it's *so* long.' Two weeks I can handle and the third week I get bored ... the fourth week, that's it and I want to come *home*.

It is the values and connections bound up in the community association that are of significance to both Jay's sense of self (including cultural and religious dimensions of her identity) and to her development of 'bonding' social capital. Similarly for Kiera, time spent at school, at church and at local Vietnamese cultural activities ultimately shaped the nature of her networks, and such spaces represented the main arenas in which she developed different forms of social capital. Unlike Jay, however, Vietnam was never seen as 'back home'. Despite visiting relatives there every few years, she lacked any real connection with her extended family and appeared indifferent about this as an aspect of her sense of self. She expressed a desire for an English name (hence her pseudonym) and during the course of the research spoke increasingly in 'street slang'. Whilst on vacation in Vietnam, her identity as an English-speaker also came to the fore:

> we [Kiera and her sister] stayed together mostly there because everyone in Vietnam tends to speak Vietnamese and we were the only two speaking English so in Vietnam we're more closer ...

Kiera and her sister's shared experience of spending much of their childhood in the UK has shaped the way they see themselves in relation to their extended family. The different spaces Jay and Kiera occupy alter their senses of self and indeed affect the relationships they seek to establish. Time was also salient. As both Jay and Kiera established more independence, their 'bridging' networks, principally developed at school, became equally and in some instances more significant than the 'bonding' social capital they created via family connections.

A spatial–temporal perspective also allows for an exploration of more covert networks. As previously highlighted, Michael's friendships were shaped fundamentally by the nature of his school and leisure activities; spaces that were purported to uphold his parents' values (Zhou 2005). During Wave One, his mother was explicit about the kinds of associations she did not wish her sons to have:

> Because to be quite honest since we moved in here we don't have children over here . . . I don't like . . . I don't want . . . . . . they don't mix with the other children.

The children to whom she referred included Christian boys whose families were also from Nigeria. Michael's life was generally highly structured and monitored, although he had been afforded some opportunities to play football in a nearby park. Much to his mother's surprise,[5] time spent within the park enabled Michael to establish a relatively covert network of local friends:

> I see quite a few people that come to the park regularly but most of them live sort of at the far back there and come from different estates around the area.

By Wave Two, however, his networks were fashioned by his acceptance of the norms and values with which he had been raised. On one school trip, for example, he demonstrated how he policed his own behaviour:

> I didn't have my parents telling me what to do so I knew what I should and shouldn't do.

Such examples illustrate both the salience of time and space and the shifting nature of young people's identities and networks.

Conclusions

This paper has sought to explore the interface between different aspects of young people's identities and the dynamic nature of their social networks. Participants' accounts have illuminated the subjective, layered, complex and dynamic nature of both identities and networks; more so than has been accounted for in many dominant social capital debates. Contrary to several influential social capital theorists, many young people *are* active in the creation of social capital *within* and *beyond* their families. It is fruitful, I believe, to view the development of social capital as an interactive process within families. As previously illustrated, Kiera and Jay's lives were shaped strongly by familial connections to cultural, ethnic and faith-based groups. Concurrently, at school they actively generated social capital that 'bridged across' different aspects of identity. Not only can familial networks be overlapping but they may also be in tension or even hidden. By shaping the spaces in which he spent much of his time, Michael's parents encouraged him to foster networks that 'bridged' across some aspects of 'difference' whilst retaining faith-based and value-oriented connections. At the same time, Michael was able to 'covertly' access alternative localized networks. Exploring young people's perspectives enables a more holistic exploration of social capital within families and communities. Further work is required to examine in more depth the inter-connections between children's and adults' social capital acquisition and identity formation over time. It would also be fruitful to develop such analyses to explore inclusionary and exclusionary practices within the context of young people's diverse and dynamic social networks.

The alternative ways in which young people understand, experience and invest in their identities and networks not only speaks volumes about the complexity of 'diversity', but also raises concerns about analyses that apply rigid categorizations to investigate, or even measure, 'bonding' or 'bridging' social capital. The use of catch-all categorizations of, for example, ethnicity and faith, can provide a pragmatic starting point for the examination of social capital and diversity. Nevertheless, a more nuanced understanding of the contexts and multiplicity of identity is fundamental. There is a danger that analyses of social capital that apply such rigid categories may fail to recognize elements of identity significant to individuals and/or collectives. Consequently, the 'unconventional' or subtle means by which individuals and communities are 'bonding' or 'bridging' may be overshadowed (see also Weller [2009]).

Time and space are both implicated in shaping the nature of identities and networks, and it is through a predominantly qualitative approach that nuances and subtleties emerge. Findings from this study, I believe, raise important questions about how notions such as 'bonding' and 'bridging' social capital might be used effectively to understand the dynamic nature of diversity and cohesion within different contexts. Such issues are paramount, given the government's commitment to embracing diversity and promoting cohesion and integration. Ultimately, policy initiatives need to be sensitive to both context and complexity in order to understand which aspects of identity *matter* in the creation and development of social capital at different times and in different spaces (see also Côté 2007).

Notes

1. Conducted by Prof. Rosalind Edwards and Dr Susie Weller.
2. For further information, please see http://www.timescapes.leeds.ac.uk.
3. This study was conducted with Prof. Irene Bruegel who, during the writing of this article, very sadly passed away.
4. Jay and her brother attended extra-curricula tuition classes covering core curriculum subjects that were coordinated by the community organization to which Jay and her family were affiliated.
5. Michael's mother, Folami, was present during both interviews.

References

BALL, S. 2003 *Class Strategies and the Education System: The Middle Class and Social Advantage*, London: Routledge-Falmer
BARKER, J. and WELLER, S. 2003 'Is it fun? Developing children centred research methods', *International Journal of Sociology & Social Policy*, vol. 23, no. 1, pp. 33–58
BASSANI, C. 2003 'Social capital theory in the context of Japanese children', *Electronic Journal of Contemporary Japanese Studies*, http://www.japanesestudies.org.uk/articles/Bassani.html (accessed 21 March 2005)
BERKELEY, R. 2002 'Foreword', in The Runnymede Trust (ed.), *Cohesion, Community and Citizenship*, London: The Runnymede Trust, pp. v–x
BONNETT, A. and CARRINGTON, B. 2000 'Fitting into categories or falling between them? Rethinking ethnic classification', *British Journal of Sociology of Education*, vol. 21, no. 4, pp. 487–500
BOURDIEU, P. 1986 'The forms of capital', in J. E. Richardson (ed.), *Handbook of Theory for Research in the Sociology of Education*, New York, NY: Greenwood Press, pp. 241–258
CABALLERO, C. EDWARDS, R. and PUTHUSSERY, S. 2008 *Parenting 'Mixed' Children: Negotiating Difference and Belonging in Mixed Race, Ethnicity and Faith Families*, York, UK: JRF
COLEMAN, J. S. 1990 *Foundations of Social Theory*, Cambridge, MA: Harvard University Press
COLEMAN, J. S., HOFFER, T. and KILGORE, S. 1982 *High School Achievement: Public, Catholic and Private Schools Compared*, New York: Basic Books
CÔTÉ, J. 2007 'Youth and the provision of resources', in H. Helve and J. Bynner (eds), *Youth and Social Capital*, London: Tufnell Press, pp. 59–70
DCSF 2008 *Education and Inspections Act 2006*, http://www.dcsf.gov.uk/publications/educationandinspectionsact/ (accessed 27 October 2008)
DUNNELL, K. 2008 *Diversity and Different Experiences in the UK: National Statistician's Annual Article on Society*, http://www.statistics.gov.uk/cci/article.asp?ID=1976 (accessed 11 September 2008)
DWYER, C. and BRESSEY, C. 2008 'Introduction: island geographies: new geographies of race and racism', in C. Dwyer and C. Bressey (eds), *New Geographies of Race and Racism*, Aldershot, UK: Ashgate, pp. 1–13

DWYER, C., MODOOD, T., SANGHERA, G., SHAH, B., and THAPAR-BJORKERT, S. 2006 'Ethnicity as social capital? Explaining the differential educational achievements of young British Pakistani men and women', Paper presented at the 'Ethnicity, Mobility and Society' Leverhulme Programme Conference at University of Bristol, 16–17 March
FIELD, J. 2003 *Social Capital*, London: Routledge
FRANKLIN, J. (ed.) 2004 'Politics, trust and networks: social capital in critical perspective', Working Paper, No. 7, Families & Social Capital ESRC Research Group, London: London South Bank University
GEORGE, R. 2007 'Urban girls' 'race' friendship and school choice: changing schools, changing friendships', *Race Ethnicity and Education*, vol. 10, no. 2, pp. 115–29
GOULBOURNE, H. and SOLOMOS, J. 2003 'Families, ethnicity and social capital', *Social Policy & Society*, vol. 2, no. 4, pp. 329–38
GRANOVETTER, M. 1973 'The strength of weak ties', *American Journal of Sociology*, vol. 78, pp. 1360–80
GRAY, A. 2003 'Towards a conceptual framework for studying time and social capital', Working Paper, No. 3, Families & Social Capital ESRC Research Group, London: London South Bank University
HELVE, H. 2007 'Social capital and minority identity', in H. Helve and J. Bynner (eds), *Youth and Social Capital*, London: Tufnell Press, pp, pp. 103–6
HELVE, H. and BYNNER, J. (eds) 2007 *Youth and Social Capital*, London: Tufnell Press
HETHERINGTON, M., BENEFIELD, P., LINES, A., PATERSON, C., RIES, J. and SHUAYB, M. 2007 Community Cohesion for Children, Young People and their Families: A Rapid Review of Policy, Practice and Research in Local Authorities, Slough: NFER
HOLLAND, J. 2008 *'Young people and social capital: What can it do for us?'* Group Working Paper, No. 24, Families & Social Capital ESRC Research, London: London South Bank University
HOLLAND, J., REYNOLDS, T. and WELLER, S. 2007 'Transitions, networks and communities: the significance of social capital in the lives of children and young people', *Journal of Youth Studies*, vol. 10, no. 1, pp. 97–116
KUUSISTO, A. 2007 'Religious identity based social networks as facilitators of teenagers' social capital: a case study on Adventist families in Finland', in H. Helve and J. Bynner (eds), *Youth and Social Capital*, London: Tufnell Press, pp. 87–102
LAWHON, T. 1997 'Encouraging friendships among children', *Childhood Education*, vol. 70, no. 7, pp. 228–34
MAND, K. and WELLER, S. 2007 'Ambivalent positions: ethnicity and working in our "own communities"', in H. Lucey and V. Gillies (eds), *Power, Knowledge and the Academy: The Institutional is Political*, Basingstoke, UK: Palgrave Macmillan, pp. 53–69
MCGONIGAL, J., DOHERTY, R., ALLAN, J., MILLS, S., CATTS, R., REDFORD, M., MCDONALD, A., MOTT, J.AND and BUCKLEY, C. 2007 'Social capital, social inclusion and changing school contexts: a Scottish perspective', *British Journal of Educational Studies*, vol. 55, no. 1, pp. 77–94
MORROW, V. 1999 'Conceptualising social capital in relation to the well-being of children and young people: a critical review', *The Sociological Review*, vol. 47, no. 4, pp. 744–65
PUTNAM, R. D. 1993 *Making Democracy Work: Civic Traditions in Modern Italy*, Princeton, NJ: Princeton University Press
PUTNAM, R. D. 2000 *Bowling Alone: The Collapse and Revival of American Community*, New York: Simon and Schuster
PUTNAM, R. D. 2007 'E pluribus unum: diversity and community in the twenty-first century', *Scandinavian Political Studies*, vol. 30, no. 2, pp. 137–74
REAY, D. and BALL, S. J. 1998 '"Spoilt for choice": the working classes and education markets', *Oxford Review of Education*, vol. 23, no. 1, pp. 89–101
REYNOLDS, T. 2007 'Judged by the company we keep: friendships networks, social capital and ethnic identity of Caribbean young people in Britain', in H. Helve and J. Bynner (eds), *Youth and Social Capital*, London: Tufnell Press, pp. 71–86

REYNOLDS, T. and ZONTINI, E. 2006 'Assessing social capital and care provision in minority ethnic communities: a comparative study of Caribbean and Italian transnational families', in R. Edwards, J. Franklin and J. Holland (eds), *Assessing Social Capital: Concept, Policy and Practice*, Newcastle, UK: Cambridge Scholars Press, pp. 217–33

SCHAEFER-MCDANIEL, N. J. 2004 'Conceptualizing social capital among young people: toward a new theory', *Children Youth and Environments*, vol. 14, no. 1, pp. 140–50

SCHULLER, T., BARON, S. and FIELD, J. 2000 'Social capital: a review and critique', in S. Baron, J. Field and T. Schuller (eds), *Social Capital: Critical Perspectives*, Oxford: Oxford University Press, pp. 1–38

SMITH, G. and KHANOM, A. 2005 *Findings: Children's Perspectives on Believing and Belonging*, York, UK: JRF

WELLER, S. 2006 'Skateboarding alone? Making social capital discourse relevant to teenagers' lives', *Journal of Youth Studies*, vol. 9, no. 5, pp. 557–74

WELLER, S. 2007a 'Managing the move to secondary school: the significance of children's social capital', in H. Helve and J. Bynner (eds), *Youth and Social Capital*, London: Tufnell Press, pp. 107–25

WELLER, S. 2007b '"Sticking with your mates?" Children's friendship trajectories during the transition from primary to secondary school', *Children & Society*, vol. 21, no. 5, pp. 339–51

WELLER, S. 2009 '"You need to have a mixed school ..." exploring the complexity of diversity in young people's social networks, in J. Allan, J. Ozga and G. Smyth (eds), *Social Capital, Professionalism and Diversity: New Relations in Urban Schools*, Rotterdam: Sense

WELLER, S. and BRUEGEL, I. 2009 'Children's "place" in the development of neighbourhood social capital', *Urban Studies*, vol. 46, no. 3, pp. 629–43

WOOLCOCK, M. 2001 'The place of social capital in understanding social and economic outcomes', *Isuma: Canadian Journal of Policy Research*, vol. 2, no. 1, pp. 1–17

ZHOU, M. 2005 'Ethnicity as social capital: community-based institutions and embedded networks of social relations', in G. C. Loury, T. Modood and S. Teles (eds), *Ethnicity, Social Mobility and Public Policy: Comparing the USA and UK*, Cambridge: Cambridge University Press, chapter 4

Index

INDEX

For Product Safety Concerns and Information please contact our EU
representative GPSR@taylorandfrancis.com
Taylor & Francis Verlag GmbH, Kaufingerstraße 24, 80331 München, Germany

www.ingramcontent.com/pod-product-compliance
Lightning Source LLC
Chambersburg PA
CBHW050521280326
41932CB00014B/2402